Digital Dictators

Media, Authoritarianism, and America's New Challenge

Edited by Ilan Berman

ROWMAN & LITTLEFIELD
Lanham • Boulder • New York • London

Published in association with The American Foreign Policy Council

Published by Rowman & Littlefield
An imprint of The Rowman & Littlefield Publishing Group, Inc.
4501 Forbes Boulevard, Suite 200, Lanham, Maryland 20706
www.rowman.com

Unit A, Whitacre Mews, 26-34 Stannary Street, London SE11 4AB

British Library Cataloguing in Publication Information Available

Library of Congress Cataloging-in-Publication Data

Library of Congress Control Number: 2018956471

ISBN 978-1-5381-1990-7 (cloth : alk. paper)
ISBN 978-1-5381-1991-4 (electronic)

This project was made possible in part through the generous support of the William H. Donner Foundation.

CONTENTS

INTRODUCTION
THE RISE OF AUTHORITARIAN MEDIA
Ilan Berman

In late 2016, in the wake of one of the most controversial presidential elections in its history, the United States unexpectedly discovered that it was embroiled in a new kind of conflict. The months that followed Republican Presidential candidate Donald J. Trump's stunning electoral victory exposed a massive Russian campaign of subversion and interference aimed at the inner workings of American democracy.

This effort, sanctioned by the Kremlin and propagated through an extensive network of official news channels, unofficial "troll factories" and private actors, can be categorized as a stunning success. It has helped to undermine trust in U.S. political institutions, which many Americans now see as compromised and vulnerable. It continues to cast a shadow over the legitimacy of the Trump administration. And it has contributed to discord within the Democratic and Republican parties as part of a national scandal that continues to profoundly roil American politics.

Such meddling, moreover, is hardly a thing of the past. As this volume goes to press, there are clear signs that the Kremlin is ramping up its disinformation efforts anew in an attempt to interfere, influence, or otherwise affect the course of the 2018 midterm elections. The U.S. intelligence community is unified in its assessment that Russia views its prior efforts as part of a larger – and still ongoing – campaign. As Director of National Intelligence Dan Coats warned Congressional lawmakers in February 2018, "[t]here should be no doubt that Russia perceives its past efforts" to disrupt the 2016 presidential campaign "as successful," or that it views the upcoming 2018 midterm elections "as a potential target for Russian influence operations."[1]

Yet so far, the United States has not mustered a coherent response to this interference. In his final public address as National Security Advisor, General H.R. McMaster told the Atlantic Council in Washington,

DC in April 2018 that the United States had "failed to impose sufficient costs" on Russia for its informational assault on democratic societies.[2] Nor has Washington used the opportunity to galvanize greater trans-Atlantic unity. Despite the fact that Russian disinformation against the U.S. is mirrored by similar campaigns directed at a host of other Western nations – including the United Kingdom, Germany, and France – a common strategy to counter this phenomenon has yet to emerge. Similarly, despite local responses now taking shape in a number of NATO countries,[3] there is as yet no Alliance-wide strategy to protect member nations from the proliferation of Russian propaganda. And because there isn't, the threat posed by such interference remains both real and enduring.

As significant as it is, however, Russia's ongoing disinformation campaign is part of a much larger challenge now confronting the United States. Recent years have seen the advent of a phenomenon that could be called "authoritarian media," entailing the weaponization of news and views, both real and fabricated, by repressive regimes and radical non-state actors via state-controlled outlets or vulnerable media platforms with the goal of advancing a discrete set of foreign policy and national security objectives.

* * * * *

Such efforts are not new, of course. Nation-states have long used propaganda, disinformation and the dissemination of selective news as a means of promoting their respective worldviews – and of diminishing those of others.

During the nearly five decades of the Cold War, the Soviet Union marshalled a massive propaganda effort (spanning cultural activities, art, movies and media) to indoctrinate its own population and to persuade foreign audiences of the superiority of Soviet ideology and the Communist system.[4] This weaponization of information – termed *dezinformatsiya* in Russian and dubbed "active measures" by Sovietologists and scholars – was remarkably successful in promoting Soviet ideals and objectives in ways that were poorly understood, and imperfectly addressed, by the West for much of the Cold War. In turn, during his nearly two decades in power, Russian President Vladimir Putin has come to embrace information warfare as an intrinsic part of his regime's extensive and ongoing "hybrid war" against the West. As the scholars Edward Lucas and Peter Pomeranzev detail, the Kremlin today has successfully harnessed "disinformation, incitement to violence and hate speech to destroy trust, sap morale, degrade the information space, erode public discourse, and increase partisanship."[5]

Communist China has similarly placed major emphasis throughout its history on mass campaigns of propaganda, adapting its methods of information dissemination to best mobilize and indoctrinate the country's large, and previously largely illiterate, population. This focus, however, is not solely internal. As experts have noted, China's ruling Communist Party has come to see "influence operations" – carried out by human agents or promulgated via extensive state information warfare – as a key strategy by which to undermine and eliminate ideological threats to its legitimacy, among them "constitutional democracy, civil society, and Western concepts of journalism."[6]

Meanwhile, in the Middle East, the advent of new media has aided and abetted a similar trend. Once an informational backwater where residents relied almost exclusively on Western or stagnant state outlets for daily news and information, the region has experienced an explosion of digital media over the past quarter-century. This transformation, in turn, has given far greater voice to some of the Middle East's most ideological actors.

Thus, the Islamic Republic of Iran has succeeded in marshalling a sprawling media effort aimed not only at enforcing its ideology domestically, but at promoting the "exportation" of its radical revolutionary strain of Shi'a Islam abroad as well, utilizing various television, radio and internet platforms. The tiny Gulf nation of Qatar, meanwhile, has become an authoritative voice in the Arab world via its infamous state broadcast channel, *Al-Jazeera*, which the country's ruling regime has used to great effect to promote Islamist ideas, as well as to undermine the credibility of the West. And in Turkey, the Islamist government of President Recep Tayyip Erdogan has launched a concerted campaign to eliminate the independence of the country's once-vibrant media sector, and to weaponize this medium for its own political ends.

Even non-state actors have moved into the ideological media space. During its heyday in the early 2000s, al-Qaeda identified the "media war" as one of the "strongest methods" for promoting its objectives, and accordingly erected a multinational multimedia conglomerate – complete with a dedicated production arm, a mouthpiece for training and operations, and dozens of websites – to assist in this effort.[7] Yet al-Qaeda's informational strategy has been dwarfed by that of its successor and ideological rival, the Islamic State (ISIS), which can be said to have truly mastered the informational domain. It has done so by disseminating sophisticated propaganda via a variety of platforms in a comprehensive "media package" that has dramatically expanded the Islamic State's appeal, recruited disaffected Muslims to its cause, and undermined the legitimacy and authority of the West.[8] This strategy (and the vision behind it) has proven remarkably compelling and is responsible for a mass mobilization of Muslims to the group's cause between 2014 and 2017, and the continued violence carried out in its name the world over since.

But if such efforts cannot be characterized as new, their scope and impact undoubtedly are, for at least two reasons. The first is the changing nature of the media sphere itself. A growing deluge of global information, in which traditional sources of media are increasingly being challenged by new (and often unreliable) information outlets, and where the proliferation of social media platforms has left users vulnerable to opaque algorithms and the biases of unaccountable editors, have undermined the traditional hierarchy and authority of established media. Second, and related, has been a "flattening" of once-authoritative sources and a fundamental rejection of established knowledge in favor of opinions that conform to selective attitudes – a phenomenon that the author Tom Nichols has termed "the death of expertise."[9]

These trends have created conditions favorable to the growth and expansion of authoritarian modes of expression. Repressive states, in turn, have taken advantage of this new, more competitive media environment to promote their own, weaponized sources of information. So, too, have non-state actors, who have gained the capacity to wage digital "guerrilla warfare" of sorts, and to do so "on their own terms and without the need for massive budgets."[10]

* * * * *

The rise of the authoritarian media phenomenon has generated important new questions and concerns for U.S. policymakers, and for the American public at large.

In his 1963 testimony before Congress, famed journalist Edward R. Murrow articulated the then-prevailing view of the "soft power" strategy that came to undergird the architecture of American public diplomacy during the decades of the Cold War. "American traditions and the American ethic require us to be truthful, but the most important reason is that truth is the best propaganda and lies are the worst," Murrow told Washington lawmakers. "To be persuasive we must believable; to be believable we must credible; to be credible we must be truthful. It is as simple as that."[11]

But is it? Is such an approach alone still sufficient today, in an era of media saturation and "fake news"? Or does the United States need a new and more assertive informational strategy in order to effectively counteract and counterbalance the broad range of authoritarian media sources and modes of disinformation that are being martialed today by authoritarian actors? And are America's existing tools of official outreach (collectively known as U.S. International Media, or USIM) equal to this task?

Similarly, what are the implications of the rise of authoritarian media for America's own attitudes toward the press? Traditionally, the American public has enjoyed a free-wheeling and largely unregulated "marketplace of ideas," based on the belief that credible news stories and reputable news sources rise to the top, while falsehoods are discredited over time. But today's "fake news" phenomenon has demonstrated the resiliency and effectiveness of such disreputable outlets and narratives – and in the process suggested that the United States government needs to take a more hands-on approach to protecting and insulating the American public from messages and programming promulgated by foreign news outlets. Indeed, recent steps (such as the Justice Department's decision, in late 2017, to force Russia's state-controlled RT channel to register as a "foreign agent"[12]) suggest that the U.S. government is already moving in this direction. But the scope and nature of such intervention is as yet poorly defined, and even more poorly regulated – giving rise to the potential for official abuse and governmental overreach.

Finally, what are the lessons of this phenomenon for America's own media sector? The U.S. "Fourth Estate" is now more politicized, and more vulnerable, than ever before. This trend is not solely a product of the global proliferation of authoritarian media, yet it has undoubtedly been amplified by it, and by the efforts of foreign actors to subvert once-reliable news outlets and sources. What steps should be taken by U.S. media outlets to preserve their integrity and ensure transparency and objectivism in the face of the authoritarian media phenomenon?

The pages that follow represent an attempt to grapple with these and other pressing questions, as well as to map the new, and challenging, media terrain that the United States will need to navigate in the years ahead.

ENDNOTES

1. As cited in Ellen Nakashima and Shane Harris, "The Nation's Top Spies said Russia is Continuing to Target the U.S. Political System," *The Washington Post*, February 13, 2018, https://www.washingtonpost.com/world/national-security/fbi-director-to-face-questions-on-security-clearances-and-agents-independence/2018/02/13/f3e4c706-105f-11e8-9570-29c9830535c5_story.html?utm_term=.4efae8fd8a36.

2. As cited in Robbie Gramer, "McMaster Unleashes on Russia in Final Speech," *Foreign Policy*, April 4, 2018, http://foreignpolicy.com/2018/04/04/mcmaster-unleashes-on-russia-in-final-speech-putin-baltic-states-hybrid-warfare-white-house-trump-national-security-advisor-failed-to-impose-costs-on-kremlin/.

3. The Czech Republic, for instance, has established a dedicated unit in its Interior Ministry to help craft an informational response to the "informational war" that Russia is waging in the country's politics. See "Czechs Set Up Unit to Counter Perceived Propaganda Threat from Russia," Reuters, October 2016, https://www.reuters.com/article/us-czech-security-russia/czechs-set-up-unit-to-counter-perceived-propaganda-threat-from-russia-idUSKCN12K22V. The Latvian government is reportedly working on a plan to expand media literacy and critical thinking in the nation's schools to make the country's youth more resistant to Russian propaganda. See Reid Standish, "Russia's Neighbors Respond to Putin's 'Hybrid War,'" *Foreign Policy*, October 12, 2017, http://foreignpolicy.com/2017/10/12/russias-neighbors-respond-to-putins-hybrid-warlatvia-estonia-lithuania-finland/.

4. For a detailed overview of the soft power informational efforts of the USSR, see Richard H. Schultz and Roy Godson, eds., *Dezinformatsiya: Active Measures in Soviet Strategy* (Washington: Pergamon Brassey's, 1984).

5. Edward Lucas and Peter Pomeranzev, *Winning the Information War: Techniques and Counter-strategies to Russian Propaganda in Central and Eastern Europe* (Center for European Policy Analysis/Legatum Institute, 2016), ii.

6. Peter Mattis, Testimony before the House Committee on Foreign Affairs, Subcommittee on Asia and the Pacific, March 21, 2018, https://docs.house.gov/meetings/FA/FA05/20180321/108056/HHRG-115-FA05-Wstate-MattisP-20180321.pdf.

7. "Letter to Mullah Mohammed 'Omar from Osama bin Laden,'" as catalogued in *Harmony and Disharmony: Exploiting Al-Qa'ida's Organizational Vulnerabilities* (New York: West Point Combating Terrorism Center, February 2006), http://ctc.usma.edu/aq/pdf/AFGP-2002-600321-Trans.pdf; Shaun Waterman, "Analysis: Al-Qaeda's Production Unit," United Press International, September 20, 2007, http://www.upi.com/Emerging_Threats/2007/09/20/Analysis_Al-Qaidas_video_production_unit/UPI-10601190302473/2/; Marc Lynch, "Al Qaeda's Media Strategy," *The National Interest.* March 1, 2006, http://www.nationalinterest.org/Article.aspx?id=11524; Gabriel Weimann, *Terror on The Internet: The New Arena, The New Challenges* (Washington, DC: United States Institute of Peace Press, 2006), 15, 67.

8. See the chapter on "The Islamic State" in *World Almanac of Islamism 2017* (Lanham: Rowman & Littlefield 2017), http://almanac.afpc.org/islamic-state.

9. See generally Tom Nichols, *The Death of Expertise: The Campaigned against Established Knowledge and Why It Matters* (Oxford University Press, 2017).

10. Haroon K. Ullah. *Digital World War: Islamists, Extremists, and the Fight for Cyber Supremacy* (New Haven, CT: Yale University Press, 2017), xvi.

11. As cited in Thomas L. McPhail, *Global Communication: Theories, Stakeholders, and Trends* (John Wiley & Sons, 2011), 90.

12. See, for example, Andrea Noble, "Russia Today Registration Part of Justice Department Crackdown on Foreign Agents Law," *The Washington Times*, November 12, 2017, https://www.washingtontimes.com/news/2017/nov/12/rt-caught-in-foreign-agents-registration-act-crack/; Jack Stubbs and Ginger Gleason, "Russia's RT America Registers as 'Foreign Agent' in U.S.," Reuters, November 13, 2017, https://www.reuters.com/article/us-russia-usa-media-restrictions-rt/russias-rt-america-registers-as-foreign-agent-in-u-s-idUSKBN1DD25B.

Russia's Disinformation Offensive
Donald N. Jensen

The Kremlin views control of information as a crucial instrument of both domestic and foreign policy. At home, Vladimir Putin systematically clamped down on internal communications – primarily television, which reaches 99 percent of the Russian population and which 73 percent of the Russian people watch daily – as well as newspapers, radio stations and the Internet.[1] At the same time, Russia's president has positioned himself as an international renegade, deploying hypermodern, contrarian media outlets like *RT* and *Sputnik*, as well as an army of online trolls, to shatter the West's monopoly on "truth."

The sweeping scope and extensive range of this campaign makes clear that the Kremlin views information as the premier weapon of the 21st century—and believes that, by adroitly harnessing it, Russia can create chaos in the international system and thereby prevail over its adversaries.[2]

Russia's Domestic Media Environment

Russia's manipulation of the media for strategic ends begins at home. By all of the metrics compiled by Freedom House, a prominent international democracy watchdog, Russia ranks as an unfree state, with an aggregate score of 20/100 (with 0 the least free and 100 the most). This illiberalism is the product of concrete, institutional arrangements and policies—some inherited from the Soviet or Yeltsin eras, others developed during Putin's rule—and a journalistic tradition in which the media has rarely operated independently of the authorities.

Even so, press freedom in Russia has declined sharply in recent years. The country's Freedom House score dropped from 60th to 83rd place between 2002 and 2015, and in relative rankings worldwide, it went from 114th to 180th place during the same period, scoring poorly in terms of its legal, political, and economic media environments.

83 Journalists Killed in Russia

between 1992 and 2018 / Motive Confirmed or Unconfirmed

CPJ

Figure 1 – Journalists killed in Russia from 1999 to 2018. Dark is "Motive Confirmed," light is "Motive Unconfirmed."[3]

Most alarming of all have been the threats to the lives of journalists, which have become increasingly common. As of April 2018, some 58 journalists had been killed since Putin's ascendance to power in 1999.[4] Attacks and arrests of members of the media are particularly high in the republic of Chechnya under the rule of local strongman Ramzan Kadyrov, who has facilitated a permissive environment for violence against journalists.[5]

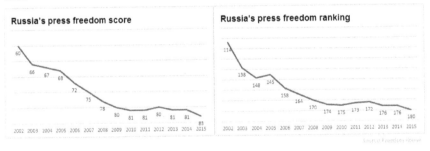

Figure 2 – Freedom House statistics on Russia's press freedom. Graph created by Politifact.[6]

Russia's domestic media environment serves as a key tool in Putin's drive to centralize power and carry out his policies. All political institutions are subservient to the Putin regime, a hold on power bolstered by a carefully controlled media environment. The result is a self-sustaining feedback loop: the regime's tight control over the media played a large role in securing Putin's reelection over the course of several electoral cycles. This, in turn, has eroded the capacity and legitimacy of Russia's political institutions and enhances the Kremlin's ability to centralize power in the name of "national cohesion."[7] This oppressive media environment marginalizes or even outright criminalizes dissent. As one Senate Foreign Relations Committee report has noted:

> Within Russia, Putin's regime has harassed and killed whistleblowers and human rights activists; crafted laws to hamstring democratic institutions; honed and amplified anti-Western propaganda; curbed media that deviate from a pro-government line; beefed up internal security agencies to surveil and harass human rights activists and journalists; directed judicial prosecutions and verdicts; cultivated the loyalties of oligarchs through corrupt handouts; and ordered violent crackdowns against protesters and purported enemies.[8]

The Kremlin keeps domestic media outlets on a short leash. It controls three of the country's most popular TV stations: NTV, ORT (now First Channel), and RTR (now Rossiya 1). General directors and editors depend on the Kremlin for their appointments, whether officially or unofficially. (The director of the state-owned corporation VGTRK, for instance, is appointed or removed by presidential decree.) As such, these outlets are not simply Kremlin-backed, but Kremlin-directed and dependent on Kremlin funding. Indeed, Putin's administration is known to hold weekly meetings with directors and editors from the mainstream broadcasters and newspapers to discuss "what will be significant in the next week, what the administration wants to cover."[9]

The regime's control over the media has allowed Putin to transform crisis points into opportunities for political centralization and cultural unification. Thus, widespread critiques of the government's handling of the year 2000 Kursk submarine disaster led to a media crackdown. Thereafter, the government mobilized the media's reaction to the 2004 terrorist attack on a Beslan school in order to replace elected regional governors with Kremlin-appointed ones. And when the 2014 invasion of Ukraine resulted in international sanctions, Russian media reinforced the "besieged fortress" narrative that attempts to legitimize Putin's actions and authority.

That year marked a turning point in the media's relationship to the Kremlin. In the immediate aftermath of Russia's annexation of Crimea, Freedom House argued that state-backed media outlets "[moved] from supporting the government with biased news to actively participating in an 'information war' with its perceived adversaries."[10] The results were succinctly summarized by *Politico*:

Russian television doesn't suggest that Russian leaders are any better or less corrupt, or more honest and just, than Western leaders. Rather, it says that everything is the same everywhere. All the world's politicians are corrupt—just look at the revelations in the Panama Papers. Everywhere, human rights are being violated—just look at what American cops do to black people. All athletes dope. All elections are falsified. Democracy doesn't exist anywhere, so give it up.[11]

Russia's independent media, whether traditional or online, now face two threats to their continued existence. The first are governmental constraints over how they operate and what narratives they can promote. The second are market pressures. Each of these considerations, in turn, exacerbates the other. The slim market share commanded by these outlets makes governmental coercion all the more effective. Independent outlets can expect to undergo regular tax inspections and criminal investigations, as with the RBC media group, whose 2016 coverage of Putin's allegedly corrupt associates in connection with the Panama Papers scandal led to legal and political pressure and the removal of the group's top editors. Several RBC journalists resigned in solidarity when the outlet was sold to a Putin ally in June 2017, and new chief editors were hired from the state-owned TASS news agency. The head of *Ekho Moskvy*, supposedly "the last remaining independent radio station," has said that "Putin is the only person who can fire him."[12]

In fact, since Putin's re-election campaign in 2011, over a dozen prominent independent outlets, both foreign and domestic, have faced resignations, restrictions, and closures as a result of Kremlin pressure, among them RIA Novosti, *Kommersant*, and *Forbes*. There are more than 400 daily newspapers, catering to most tastes, but the most popular titles support official policy. Several influential dailies have been bought by companies with close links to the Kremlin. Access to diverse points of view is further limited because independent foreign broadcasters such as RFE/RL and the *Voice of America* face severe restrictions on their work. A law which came into force in 2016 caps foreign ownership of media outlets at 20 percent. Since then, many foreign companies have either quit the market or ceded majority control of their Russian operations to local partners.[13]

Russia's internet penetration rate stands at 76.4 percent, a fraction higher than that of the United States. While still less tightly controlled than traditional media, the Kremlin has made moves to restrict online freedoms in recent years. Facing major antigovernment protests across Russia in 2017 – which many observers, including the Kremlin, saw as having been fueled by social media – and a presidential election in March 2018, authorities scrambled to more strictly monitor online content and strengthen legal regulation.

	2016	2017
Internet Freedom Status	Not Free	Not Free
Obstacles to Access (0-25)	10	11
Limits on Content (0-35)	23	23
Violations of User Rights (0-40)	32	32
TOTAL* (0-100)	**65**	**66**

* 0=most free, 100=least free

Population:	144.3 million
Internet Penetration 2016 (ITU):	76.4 percent
Social Media/ICT Apps Blocked:	Yes
Political/Social Content Blocked:	Yes
Bloggers/ICT Users Arrested:	Yes
Press Freedom 2017 Status:	Not Free

Figure 3 - Freedom House, "Freedom on the Net," 2017[14]

The results have been a dramatically constrained operating environment online for Russian internet outlets and activists, as well as for ordinary citizens. Internet stories running counter to official narratives on Moscow's involvement in Crimea and in Syria, among other issues, often result in website blocking or prison sentences.[15] Social media users and journalists have been jailed for their online comments. This has included LGBTQ activists, who were charged with spreading "propaganda of nontraditional sexual relations" and ordered to pay hefty fines, while other users have been punished for posting material deemed offensive to religious believers.[16]

Moreover, recent laws have curtailed the online anonymity of Russian citizens, making virtual private networks (VPNs) that mask IP addresses harder to use. In order to access messaging apps, users are now required to disclose their phone numbers, and therefore their identities, ahead of time.

Other regulations also abound. A 2015 law required tech firms, both domestic and foreign, to store data about Russian citizens within Russia itself.[17] In November 2016, the decision to block business networking website LinkedIn for failing to comply with data localization served as a warning to other foreign companies.[18] Meanwhile, Internet Service Providers (ISPs) face hefty fines if they do not block blacklisted sites.[19] Since 2013, the state telecom regulator, ROSKOMNADZOR, has the power to block any websites that "disseminate calls for riots, 'extremist' activities, or participation in illegal assemblies." According to the human rights NGO Roskomsvoboda, by mid-2016 Russian authorities had blocked over 30,000 websites under these parameters.[20]

SOWING CHAOS ABROAD

For all of Russia's weaknesses as a great power, Putin believes that it has one key advantage in its long-term competition with the United States and NATO: that Russia is more cohesive internally, and thus able to outlast its technologically-superior but culturally- and politically-pluralistic opponents. In recent years, the Kremlin has used coercion, misinformation and other disruptive strategies to spread chaos, with the goal of creating an environment in which the side that copes best with such chaos (that is, the one which is less susceptible to societal disruption) wins. In other words, Putin believes that Russia can endure in a clash of civilizations by splintering its opponents' alliances, dividing adversaries internally, and undermining their political systems while consolidating its own population, resources, and cultural base. Such a strategy avoids competing in those areas where Russia is weak in hopes of ensuring that, when confrontation does come, Russia will enjoy a more level playing field.

Russian assessments of the international system make it clear that the Kremlin considers the country to be engaged in full-scale information warfare. This is reflected in Russia's most recent military doctrine, which was approved in December of 2014,[21] in statements by Russian officials and experts,[22] and in Moscow's aggressive use of influence operations abroad. Crucial elements of an open society – such as TV channels, social media, civic groups, political parties or economic actors – now regularly serve as the Kremlin's weapons in the spread of disinformation. Unlike during the Cold War, today's Russian propaganda does not just crudely promote the Kremlin's foreign policy agenda. Rather, today's efforts to manipulate the information space through the spread of "disinformation" are intended to use the openness of Western systems against them.[23]

The Kremlin sees information warfare as but one weapon in a wide-ranging arsenal – one that includes energy, money, cultural ties, and even the Russian Orthodox Church – to be used to serve its foreign policy objectives elsewhere, especially against the United States and its European allies. These goals include reducing the role of the United States on the European continent, weakening NATO and the European Union, disrupting the political processes of Western democracies, and strengthening Russia's influence in the states along its periphery, often by claiming a "responsibility to protect" ethnic Russians outside the Russian Federation.[24]

Examples of Russia's information strategy in action are numerous. In the Baltic States, modern Russian disinformation tries to exploit fears of U.S. abandonment, while simultaneously stoking feelings of alienation among local populations. In Romania, Russia foments animosity toward Western "meddling" and eats away at public faith in NATO. In countries like Ukraine, where Russian interests are particularly extensive, Moscow tried to incite and exploit ethnic and linguistic feelings to create a prelude for a land-grab. It is Russian disinformation that has attempted to cultivate anti-Ukrainian sentiments among the Polish population, and widened internal and public cleavages in Lithuania over energy diversification policies. Facts have become disfigured. Policy debates have become diverted. NATO has become the "enemy" in some corners. Publics are left dismayed, suspicious or inert. Euro-Atlantic solidarity erodes. Yet disinformation is only a *means*. Chaos is the *aim*.

THE MODERN MEANS OF RUSSIAN DISINFORMATION

The Russian practice of information warfare combines a number of tried and tested tools of influence with a new embrace of modern technology and capabilities such as the internet. Some underlying objectives, guiding principles and state activity are broadly recognizable as reinvigorated aspects of subversion campaigns dating back to the Cold War era and even earlier. But Russia also has invested extensively in updating the principles of subversion.[25]

These new investments cover three main areas: internally and externally focused media with a substantial online presence (*RT* and *Sputnik* are the best known of these outlets); the use of social media (especially online discussion boards and comment pages) as a force multiplier to ensure Russian narratives achieve broad reach and penetration; and language skills necessary to engage with target audiences on a wide front. The result is a presence in many countries acting in coordination with Moscow-backed media and the Kremlin itself. It should be emphasized that the Russian information campaigns visible to an English-language audience are only part of a broad front covering multiple languages, including not only state-backed media and trolling, but also "false flag" media—sock puppet websites set up to resemble genuine news outlets, which seed their news feeds with false or contentious reporting that ties in with

Russian narratives. This "false flag" approach extends to *RT* determinedly masquerading as a broadcaster, and to cloning accounts on social media in order to mimic and discredit genuine Western media outlets.[26]

Externally Focused Media

State-owned *RT* (previously *Russia Today*) is perhaps the most prominent mechanism by which Russia disseminates disinformation abroad. The channel plays a critical role in shaping the online and broadcast international media environment, either by openly spreading narratives in host countries' native languages, or by laundering Kremlin narratives through local, "independent" proxy media. *RT* is particularly well-placed to accomplish this. It has a $300 million budget, online platforms with high visibility on social media and dozens of foreign-based stations broadcasting in no fewer than six languages: Arabic, English, French, German, Russian, and Spanish. Much of its online content has also been translated into various Eastern European languages. In this way, *RT* perpetuates the illusion that multiple, seemingly unconnected outlets have come to identical conclusions. *RT*'s editor-in-chief, Margarita Simonyan, has direct connections with the Kremlin. According to Simonyan, allegations that *RT* serves as a Putin mouthpiece amount to nothing more than "McCarthyism." Yet, as Putin himself said, *RT* and related platforms exist to "break the monopoly of the Anglo-Saxon global information streams."[27]

Thus, *RT* reporters are steered towards pro-Russia analytical "angles." They are warned against straying from the channel's Kremlin-backed editorial line, which is maintained by managers rather than editors. ("That phrase 'our angle' came up in staff discussions constantly," said one former employee.[28]) Many of these Russian reporters, hired for their English fluency, appear "apathetic or apolitical, with no prior experience in journalism," which cuts against the effectiveness of *RT*'s large budget and larger ambitions.[29] American and British reporters are hired directly out of journalism school, with many of these inexperienced workers receiving six-figure salaries for five days' work every two weeks.[30] Meanwhile, more experienced foreign staff sometimes find themselves marginalized: when some foreign journalists protested how *RT* had been covering Ukraine, management simply took them off the assignment and handed it to Russian staff instead.

"*RT* is unreformable," a former employee told *The Moscow Times*. "Our attempt to change *RT*, to make it more professional and objective, would likely have just made it a more effective propaganda medium. I am glad that a combination of apathy, a lack of professionalism and a dearth of real talent keep *RT* from being more effective than it currently is."[31] But not all *RT* content is noticeably biased. As Misha Glenny, author of the book *McMafia*, argues, "The Russians have moved on since the days of Pravda, the Soviet Communist party newspaper, or Radio Moscow International during the cold war. At least then you knew it was all guff, coming out of the Ideological Secretariat. RT is designed to confuse and muddy the waters. That mixture of genuine and guff leaves you baffled and disoriented, which, I guess, is the point."[32]

Also of significance is *Sputnik*. Since November 2014, the state-owned international network has employed a varied array of disinformation tools, such as social media, news outlets, and radio content. *Sputnik* operates in 31 different languages, has a $69 million annual budget, and maintains 4.5 million Facebook followers (by contrast, *RT* has 22.5 million). Its primary purpose, much like that of *RT*, is to "ping pong" unreliable information, suspect stories, and pro-Russian narratives from marginal news sites into more mainstream outlets (See Appendix I). As such, despite relatively low readership as compared to mainstream media, *Sputnik* has proven useful for Moscow's interests. *Sputnik* orders its journalists to pursue conspiracy theories that have already been discredited, such as the July 2016 death of Democratic National Committee staffer Seth Rich (which Russian sources have suggested was an internal political assassination), the notion that Russians were not involved in the leak of DNC documents to WikiLeaks in 2016, and even "unfounded rumors about the sexual preferences of the pro-EU candidate, Emmanuel Macron" during the 2017 French presidential election.[33]

Social Media

Cyber activities in the broad sense are critical to Russia's offensive disinformation campaigns – whether establishing sources for disinformation by setting up false media outlets online, or by using social media to address targets of opportunity for subversion and destabilization efforts. These activities are augmented by the ubiquitous activities of trolls (online profiles run by humans) and bots (profiles run by automated processes), which exploit specific features of the relationship between traditional and social media in order to plant, disseminate and lend credibility to disinformation.

The large amount of resources devoted to doing so stems from the recognition that digital media are becoming the main – and for a growing number of young people, the only – channel for political information and communication. They are the primary space for political activities, where citizens receive political information, shape their political views and beliefs, and have the opportunity to influence the processes related to the functioning of power. Russia's cyber activities consequently also capitalize on the fact that new social media have become the most effective tool for influencing the minds of huge communities, even entire nations.[34]

Another related campaign – and one that is commonly underestimated – entails the use of false accounts posing as authoritative information sources on social media. The Twitter accounts @Vaalit ("Elections" in Finnish) and @EuroVaalit look at first sight like innocent, and possibly even official, sources of election information, and no doubt many people, without looking closely, take them for precisely that. In fact, however, they and a range of associated accounts repeat Russian disinformation, and their profiles link to *RT*. Multiply this approach by many different languages, countries and campaigns, and factor in Russian successes in closing down opposing social media accounts as described above, and the cumulative effect cannot be other than highly corrosive.[35]

MIXED IMPACT

Russia's authoritarian media enjoy some superficial advantages as a competitive international strategy. First, the Kremlin does not need to beat its Western competitors outright – only to keep them confused, uncoordinated and off balance. Second, Russia's leaders believe that their authoritarian system grants them a natural competitive advantage in managing the psychology and politics of disorder. A third advantage is stealth; Russia's disinformation (and associated cyber) operations – a prime vehicle for seeding division and distraction – leverage the anonymity, immediacy and ubiquity of the digital age. Thus, as seen in recent Western elections, Russia regularly catches the West off guard.

But there are disadvantages as well. Russia's information strategy could backfire: efforts at sowing instability in a neighbor's lands can have a boomerang effect, generating instability that eventually affects Russia itself. In the lead-up to World War I, for example, Russia employed an aggressive information warfare campaign aimed at splintering Austria-Hungary and undermining it as a unified actor. The effort spread instability in Russia's own western regions and contributed to a surge of Bolshevism that forced Russia out of the war. Indeed, in today's war against Ukraine, Russia has sealed its borders against returning fighters lest they cause trouble at home.[36]

Another problem with the purposeful use of disinformation is that it becomes inherently more escalatory with time. Subversive moves that are initially surreptitious become more recognizable with use. Since they are ultimately a part of war, it is hard to know when disinformation campaigns are a prelude to more kinetic operations. The preparations and counter-moves that they prompt on the part of their targets can trigger tests of strength, the avoidance of which was the starting aim of the strategy.

Judged by these standards, the record of Russia's authoritarian media in achieving the Kremlin's foreign policy objectives has been mixed. In some cases, Russia's information policies have had tangible impact. Within Central and Eastern European countries in particular, Russia has successfully exploited "the bitter memories of past territorial disputes, nationalist-secessionist tendencies, and the haunting specters of chauvinist ideologies promising to make these nations great again."[37] In January 2016, the infamous German "Lisa" case, in which a Russian-language channel incorrectly reported that migrants had sexually assaulted a 13-year-old German girl, led to massive anti-immigrant and anti-Merkel protests even after the story, which was amplified through *RT* and *Sputnik*'s German- and English-language outlets, had been disproven.[38] More recently, Germany's far-right, anti-immigrant, and Kremlin-friendly Alternative for Deutschland (AfD) party received favorable coverage of its candidates and narratives in the run-up to Germany's September 2017 election, which may have helped it become Germany's third-largest party.[39] Favorable *Sputnik* coverage also may have boosted the showing of the pro-Moscow populist parties, the Five-star Movement and Lega Nord, in the recent Italian elections.[40]

During the 2016 U.S. presidential election campaign, the effectiveness of Russian trolls at reaching voters prompted some U.S. businesses to hire them to run favorable material for $25 to $50 per post. One former troll told *RFE/RL* that employees at a St. Petersburg troll factory were required to remain on duty 24/7, activated for 12-hour shifts, with a daily quota of 135 comments at least 200 characters long on topics and keywords assigned each day.[41] Some salaries were as high as $1,400 per week, another former employee told the *New York Times* in 2018. "They were just giving me money for writing," he said. "I was much younger and did not think about the moral side. I simply wrote because I loved writing. I was not trying to change the world."[42] By mid-2015, the staff had grown from a few dozen to over 1,000, a cost-effective means of reshaping the global social media landscape, without the need to necessarily recruit fully committed ideologues.[43]

Kremlin-backed media can, moreover, prove crucial during political crises. During and after the 2014 annexation of Crimea, Russian propaganda portrayed the February revolution in Kiev as all too willing to ally with fascists during the course of its "illegal" coup – which was, in the end, a Western front, as evidenced (according to *RT* and *Sputnik*) by the quick support extended to Ukraine by Europe and the United States after the ouster of pro-Kremlin premier Viktor Yanukovych. But not all favorable narratives were cooked up in Moscow. Some Western media outlets and even think tanks unwittingly advance the Kremlin's cause when they overemphasize Ukraine's internal split between a supposedly pro-European western half of the country and the pro-Russian east, ostensibly the inevitable product of linguistic, religious or ethnic divisions.

The most effective technique for Kremlin media appears to be the use of cluster narratives, which bundle multiple, even contradictory arguments together (See Appendix I). According to experimental research compiled by RAND, this "firehose" propaganda model is effective due to the variety, volume, and views of sources.[44] First, people are more likely to accept information when it is received through a *variety* of sources, despite ostensibly coming from different perspectives or different arguments which promote the same conclusions. Second, the persuasiveness of a message is more dependent on the *number* of arguments made than on their quality. Endorsements from large numbers of other readers (even bots) boosts an individual's trust in the information received. Third, views from propaganda sources are more persuasive when the recipient identifies with the source, whether in terms of ethnicity, language, nationality, ideology or other factors. "Credibility can be social," RAND finds, as "people are more likely to perceive a source as credible if others" do too.[45]

These three factors interact in complex ways. For instance, when the volume of information about a subject is high, people favor views from other users instead of experts (as when the information volume is low). The variety and number of these generally untrustworthy sources has significant bearing on their trust in the message received. Overall, however, it is clear that the greater the volume of propaganda, and the more sources available, the more effective Russian disinformation campaigns are at drowning out alternative messages and increasing the exposure and perceived credibility of their preferred narratives.[46]

On the other hand, the audience for *RT* is often overstated by the

Kremlin, deliberately obscuring the difference between reach and audience. *RT* claims it reaches 500-700 million viewers across 100 countries, but in 2015 *The Daily Beast* found that this reflected "just the theoretical geographical scope of the audience," not an actual assessment of *RT*'s real viewers.[47] *RT* and *Sputnik* combined are only watched by 2.8 percent of people in Moldova, 1.3 percent in Belarus, and 5.3 percent of Serbians, according to BBG data from June 2017.[48] In the U.S., *RT America* has been forced to register as a foreign agent, which means it must disclose financial information to the U.S. government.[49] *RT*'s UK channel has been reprimanded by telecom regulator OFCOM more than a dozen times for its skewed, false reporting.[50] Yet this official attention stands in stark contrast with *RT*'s actual influence. In Britain, *RT*'s broadcast reach is limited, hovering at around 413,000 viewers weekly, as compared to 4.4 million for *Sky News* and 7.3 million for *BBC News*.[51] In the U.S., despite programs made by well-known figures such as Larry King, *RT* is "largely absent" in the Nielsen rankings. In Europe, its 2013 TV viewership totaled less than 0.1 percent of the continent's total audience.

    RT's social media is far more successful than its broadcasting arm. Yet despite high online viewership on YouTube and other sites, 81 percent of views on *RT*'s top 100 most watched videos went to content of "natural disasters, accidents, crime and natural phenomena."[52] Its politics and current events videos represented just one percent of its overall YouTube exposure.[53] Pushback from the U.S. government and U.S. corporations may have reduced Russia's online disinformation capabilities even further. In October 2017, Twitter decided it would no longer allow paid advertisements from *RT* and *Sputnik*. A month later, in an implicit attempt to "derank" *RT* and *Sputnik* from search results, Google's parent company Alphabet announced it had "adjusted [their] signals to help surface more authoritative pages and demote low-quality content."[54] Even when accounting for Russian propaganda's actual audience, as opposed to its potential reach, most viewers and readers gravitate toward non-political content anyway. Though the Kremlin's goal is to steer *RT*'s audience from such content toward Russian disinformation more broadly, there is little evidence that this strategy has much success. Still, the international goal of Russian state media actors is not simply to boost ratings, but rather to spread disinformation narratives favorable to the Kremlin. The two are not always the same, as narratives and false facts can "ping pong" between outlets, amplified through coordinated social media targeting or just good fortune.

    Elsewhere, the diffuse, uncoordinated and self-regulating nature of social media sometimes has facilitated effective self-defense mechanisms. A new alertness to the prevalence of orchestrated troll campaigns has led to the dissemination of self-help guides for dealing with trolls in some nations. The growing availability of tools for detection of the less sophisticated troll and bot campaigns through technical and quantitative analysis is assisting in spreading awareness. As a result, according to one Russian assessment, despite the "billions of dollars" spent by the Russian state in an attempt to "turn social networks into its obedient weapon," internet society has begun to develop an immunity.[55]

THE EVOLVING THREAT

The disinformation tools used by Moscow against the West are still fairly basic. They rely on exploiting human gullibility, vulnerabilities in the social media ecosystem, and a lack of awareness among the public, the media, and policymakers. However, Russian information war capability is not a static project. Rather, it is dynamic, and is constantly developing new approaches not yet reflected in mainstream reporting or popular awareness. It is adaptable to changing political landscapes and technological advancements. In the very near term, moreover, technological advancements in artificial intelligence and cyber capabilities will open opportunities for malicious actors to undermine democracies more covertly and effectively than what we have seen to date.[56]

Indeed, Russia has begun of late fto experiment with two new disinformation strategies.

Less detectible, more targeted computational propaganda. At present, automated accounts can often be tracked easily, given sufficient time and manpower. Though designed to blend in with genuine human conversations, bots "depend on human curation and... are deployed in predictable patterns."[57] Multiple accounts, perhaps even thousands of them, are turned on at once, and their repetitive content (spreading human-generated content from outlets like *RT*) is published at "non-human speeds."

Soon, however, automated bots and fake accounts will become "increasingly sophisticated at mimicking human behavior" without human direction, using AI to adapt to new developments and generate new content at a rapid pace, if not in real time. They will even improve interactions with human users by analyzing their available data to automatically produce micro-targeted messaging designed to produce specific emotional responses and political opinions. As such, bots and users may become indistinguishable from one another, which would allow the Kremlin to sow distrust and launder narratives with greater effectiveness.[58] This potential to generate user-specific messages represents the culmination of a propagandistic dream: narratives individually tailored for each and every person, much like advertisements made personal for every customer.[59]

Enhanced video content and deepfakes. Among the Kremlin's many threat vectors in recent years, video-manipulated propaganda has been notably absent, despite the fact that in 2013 *RT* became the first news site to reach one billion views on YouTube, and it currently has 2.5 million subscribers. Millions of Western voters, young and old, rely on YouTube and other platforms for information, opinions, and current events. "More than half of American adults say they watch YouTube," Senator Mark Warner (D-VA) warned, making it a "target-rich environment for any disinformation campaign." [60] But so far, Moscow largely relies on traditional disinformation tactics when it comes to video. In the future, therefore, Russian disinformation may pivot towards video.

Since January 2018, the internet has experienced a surge in so-called "deepfakes": videos, mostly pornographic, manipulated to replace the original faces with someone else's (usually that of a famous actress). Programs such as FakeApp have emerged to make this previously laborious technique user-friendly. With enough images of a celebrity's face and an existing video in hand, an app can render a short deepfake video within 48 hours.[61] (Comparable audio manipulation already exists; the Lyrebird program can extract a "digital voice" with as little as a minute of audio input). The implicates are obvious. Soon, "political leaders can be made to appear to say anything at all, and they will sound and look exactly as they do in real life... If the viewers cannot trust their eyes and ears, confidence in media could plummet even further."[62] Thus, videos of Russian wrongdoing can be altered, while innocuous videos of Kremlin opponents, both at home and abroad, can turn into widely-shared, convincing fakes. Eventually, this manipulation will be not only automated, but micro-targeted as well, with subjects digitally manipulated to say or do whatever is most likely to generate the desired response.

ADDRESSING RUSSIAN MEDIA

The "shock and awe" of Putin's propaganda campaign has certainly been impressive, but it has also been distracting. Up to now, a great deal of the Western response to Russia's non-linear strategy has centered on highly specific aspects—such as what the Kremlin's "bots" are doing, or how a specific hashtag went viral. This emphasis on the immediacy of Russia's conduct has created a pattern of constant *reaction* on the part of the United States and its international partners. What is missing is an ability to better *anticipate* Russia's next moves.[63]

By recognizing how the constituent parts – or methods – of Russia's approach to information warfare form a holistic non-linear strategy, Western leaders might be less susceptible to continual surprise from Moscow. Developing a better understanding of what Russia is attempting in the first place is a useful next step in calibrating such responses. Learning from what is already being done by Russia's modern-day targets (e.g., in the Baltic States, Poland and Ukraine) is another. The organizing aim in this process should be to improve the West's strategic advantage in the competition of disorder now underway with the Kremlin.[64]

Appendix I: The Kremlin's Disinformation Techniques
Source: Center for European Policy Analysis
http://infowar.cepa.org/Techniques

Disinformation and new propaganda can take many forms—from the use of false visuals or misleading headlines, to social media techniques that create an impression that the "majority" understands an issue in a certain way. In the echo chamber of the modern information space, the spreading of disinformation is as easy as a "like," "tweet," or a "share." The following are some of the Kremlin's most commonly used techniques for spreading false stories and disinformation:

Ping pong – The coordinated use of complementary websites to springboard a story into mainstream circulation.

Wolf cries wolf – The vilification of an individual or institution for something you also do.

Misleading title – Facts or statements in the article are correct, or mostly correct, but the title is misleading.

No proof – Facts or statements that are not backed up with proof or sources.

Card stacking – Facts or statements are partially true. This occurs when information is correct, but it is offered selectively, or key facts are omitted. The Kremlin typically uses this technique to guide audiences to a conclusion that fits into a pre-fabricated or false narrative.

False facts – Facts or statements are false. For example, an interview mentioned in an article that never took place, or an event or incident featured in a news story that did not actually occur.

False visuals – A variant of false facts, this technique employs the use of fake or manipulated provocative visual material. Its purpose is to lend extra credibility to a false fact or narrative.

Denying facts – A variant of "false facts," this occurs when real facts are denied or wrongly undermined. The facts of an event might be reported, but an attempt is made to discredit their veracity. Alternatively, the facts may be re-interpreted to achieve the same effect: to establish doubt among an audience over the validity of a story or narrative.

Exaggeration and over-generalization – This method dramatizes. raises false alarms or uses a particular premise to shape a conclusion. A related technique is *totum pro parte.*

Totum pro parte – The "whole for a part." An example: portraying the views of a single journalist or expert as the official view or position of a government.

Changing the quotation, source or context – Facts and statements are reported from other sources, but they are now different than the original or do not account for the latest editorial changes. For example, a quotation is correct, but the person to whom it is attributed has changed, or a quote's context is altered so as to change its meaning or significance in the original story.

Loaded words or metaphors – Using expressions and metaphors to support a false narrative or hide a true one; for example, using a term like "mysterious death" instead of "poisoning" or "murder" to describe the facts of a story.

Ridiculing, discrediting, diminution – Marginalizing facts, statements or people through mockery, name-calling (i.e., *argumentum ad hominem*), or by undermining their authority. This includes using traditional and new media humor, in order to discredit on non-substantive merits.

Whataboutism – Using false comparisons to support a pre-fabricated narrative or justify deeds and policies; i.e., "We may be bad, but others are just as bad" or, "The annexation of Crimea was just like the invasion of Iraq." This technique is often accompanied by an *ad hominem* attack.

Narrative laundering – Concealing and cleaning the provenance of a source or claim. When a so-called expert of dubious integrity presents false facts or narratives as the truth. Often, this happens when propaganda outlets mimic the format of mainstream media. A common technique is to feature a guest "expert" or "scholar" on a TV program whose false fact or narrative can then be repackaged for wider distribution. For example, "Austrian media writes that..." or "A well-known German political expert says that..."

Exploiting balance – This happens when otherwise mainstream media outlets try to "balance" their reporting by featuring professional propagandists or faux journalists and experts. The effect is to inject an otherwise legitimate news story or debate with false facts and narratives. This technique is common in televised formats, which feature point-counterpoint debates. Propagandists subsequently hijack a good-faith exchange of opposing views.

Presenting opinion as facts (and vice-versa) – An opinion is presented as a fact in order to advance or discredit a narrative.

Conspiracy theories – Employing rumors, myths or claims of conspiracy to distract or dismay an audience. Examples include: "NATO wants to invade Russia;" "The United States created the Zika virus;" "Secret Baltic agencies are infecting Russian computers with viruses" or "Latvia wants to send its Russian population to concentration camps." A variation of this technique is conspiracy in reverse—or attempting to discredit a factual news story by labeling it a conspiracy.

Joining the bandwagon – Creating the impression that the "majority" prefers or understands an issue in a certain way. The majority's presumed wisdom lends credence to a conclusion or false narrative; e.g., "People are asking...," "People want..." or "People know best."

False dilemma – Forcing audiences into a false binary choice, typically "us" vs. "them."

Drowning facts with emotion – A form of the "appeal to emotion" fallacy, this is when a story is presented in such an emotional way that facts lose their importance. An example is the "Lisa case," in which Muslim immigrants in Germany were falsely reported to have sexually assaulted a Russian girl. While the event was entirely fabricated, its appeal to emotion distracted audiences from the absence of facts. Common variants of this method evoke post-Soviet nostalgia across Central and Eastern Europe, or stoke public fear of nuclear war.

Creating the context – Most commonly found on broadcast news programs, it creates the context for a pre-fabricated narrative by preceding and following a news story in such a way that it changes the meaning of the news itself. For example, in order to send the message that recent terrorist attacks in Europe were the result of EU member states not working with Russia – which is helping to fight ISIS in Syria – commentary broadcast before the news on the March 2016 Brussels attacks described Russia's success in Syria and its ability to fight ISIS effectively.

ENDNOTES

1. "Top 10 Russia's Media in 2014," russiansearchtips.com, n.d., https://www.russiansearchtips.com/2015/01/top-10-russias-largest-media-2014/.
2. Jill Dougherty, "How the Media Became One of Putin's Most Powerful Weapons," *The Atlantic*, April 21, 2015, https://www.theatlantic.com/international/archive/2015/04/how-the-media-became-putins-most-powerful-weapon/391062/.
3. Committee to Protect Journalists, "58 Journalists Killed in Russia between 1992 and 2018 : Motive Confirmed," n.d., https://cpj.org/data/killed/europe/russia/?status=Killed&motiveConfirmed%5B%5D=Confirmed&type%5B%5D=Journalist&cc_fips%5B%5D=RS&start_year=1992&end_year=2018&group_by=year.
4. Ibid.
5. International Federation of Journalists, "Deaths of Journalists in Russia," n.d., https://web.archive.org/web/20110819032825/http://journalists-in-russia.org/journalists/index/federaldistrict-plus%3AChechnya.
6. Linda Qiu, "Does, Vladimir Putin Kill Journalists?" politifact.com, January 4, 2016, http://www.politifact.com/punditfact/article/2016/jan/04/does-vladimir-putin-kill-journalists/.
7. Peter Baker, "Putin Moves to Centralize Authority," *Washington Post*, September 14, 2004, http://www.washingtonpost.com/wp-dyn/articles/A17838-2004Sep13.html.
8. "Putin's Asymmetric Assault on Democracy in Russia And Europe: Implications for U.S. National Security," Minority Staff Report Prepared for the Use of the Committee on Foreign Relations, United States Senate, January 19, 2018, 15, https://www.foreign.senate.gov/imo/media/doc/FinalRR.pdf.
9. Ekine Gordts, "Putin's Press: How Russia's President Controls the News," *Huffington Post*, October 24, 2015, https://www.huffingtonpost.com/entry/vladimir-putin-russia-news-media_us_56215944e4b0bce34700b1df.
10. Freedom House, "Freedom of the Press: 2015," 2015, https://freedomhouse.org/report/freedom-press/2015/russia.
11. Mikhail Zygar, "Why Putin Prefers Trump," *Politico*, July 27, 2015, https://www.politico.com/magazine/story/2016/07/don-

ald-trump-vladimir-putin-2016-214110.

12. Gordts, "Putin's Press."

13. "Russia Profile – Media," BBC News, April 25, 2017, http://www.bbc.com/news/world-europe-17840134.

14. Freedom House, "Freedom on the Net: 2017," 2017, https://freedomhouse.org/report/freedom-net/2017/russia.

15. Ibid.

16. Ibidem.

17. Ibidem.

18. Donald N. Jensen, "The Kremlin Target Encrypted Messaging," Center for European Policy Analysis, October 24, 2017, http://infowar.cepa.org/EN/Kremlin-targets-encrypted-messaging.

19. Freedom House, "Freedom on the Net: 2017."

20. Ibid.

21. *Military Doctrine of the Russian Federation*, approved December 26, 2014, http://news.kremlin.ru/media/events/files/41d-527556bec8deb3530.pdf.

22. See "'Информационные войны с самими собой [Information wars with themselves],'" *Postimees-DZD*, November 7, 2011, http://rus.postimees.ee/624820/informacionnye-vojny-s-samimi-soboj. See also Greg Simons, "Perception of Russia's soft power and influence in the Baltic States," *Public Relations Review* 41, iss. 1, March 2015, http://www.sciencedirect.com/science/article/pii/S0363811114001623. For another assessment of the development of modern Russian information warfare from its historical roots, see Maria Zaitseva, "Information and security components of the Russian foreign policy," *Informacijos mokslai* no. 70, 2014, 58–68.

23. For more, see Donald N. Jensen, "Russia in the Middle East: A New Front in the Information War?" Jamestown Foundation, December 20, 2017, https://jamestown.org/program/russia-middle-east-new-front-information/.

24. Vladimir Baranovsky and Anatoly Mateiko, "Responsibility to Protect: Russia's Approaches," *International Spectator* 51, iss. 2, 2016, https://www.tandfonline.com/doi/abs/10.1080/03932729.2016.1176648?journalCode=rspe20.

25. Keir Giles, "Russia's 'New' Tools for Confronting the West," Chatham House *Research Paper*, March 2016, 27-28, https://www.chathamhouse.org/sites/files/chathamhouse/publications/2016-03-russia-new-tools-giles.pdf.

26. Ibid.

27. Jim Rutenberg, "RT, Sputnik and Russia's New Theory of War," *New York Times*, September 13, 2017, https://www.nytimes.com/2017/09/13/magazine/rt-sputnik-and-russias-new-theory-of-war.html.

28. "Welcome to The Machine: Inside the Secretive World of RT," *The Moscow Times*, June 1, 2017, https://themoscowtimes.com/articles/welcome-to-the-machine-inside-the-secretive-world-of-rt-58132.

29. Ibid.

30. Tim Dowling, "24-hour Putin People: My Week Watching Kremlin 'Propaganda Channel' RT," *Guardian* (London), November 29, 2017, https://www.theguardian.com/media/2017/nov/29/24-hour-putin-people-my-week-watching-kremlin-propaganda-channel-rt-russia-today.

31. "Welcome to The Machine."

32. As cited in Dowling, "24-hour Putin people."

33. "Putin's Asymmetric Assault on Democracy in Russia And Europe: Implications for U.S. National Security," 43.

34. Giles, "Russia's 'New' Tools for Confronting the West," 44-45.

35. Ibid., 46.

36. Donald N. Jensen, "Moscow in the Donbas: Command, Control, Crime and the Minsk Peace Process," NATO Defense College *Research Report*, March 2017, http://www.ndc.nato.int/news/news.php?icode=1029.

37. Alina Polyakova and Spencer P. Bouer, *The Future of Political Warfare: Russia, the West, and the Future of Global Digital Competition* (Brookings, March 2018), https://www.brookings.edu/wp-content/uploads/2018/03/fp_20180316_future_political_warfare.pdf.

38. Ibid.

39. Simon Shuster, "How Russian Voters Fueled the Rise of Germany's Far-Right," *TIME*, September 25, 2017, http://time.com/4955503/germany-elections-2017-far-right-russia-angela-merkel/.

40. Donald N. Jensen, "The Italian Elections Open the Door toward Russia Wider," Center for European Policy Analysis, March 20, 2018, http://infowar.cepa.org/EN/Italian-elections-open-the-door-toward-Russia-wider.

41. "One Professional Troll Tells All," *Radio Free Europe/Radio Lib-*

erty, March 25, 2015, https://www.rferl.org/a/how-to-guide-russian-trolling-trolls/26919999.html.

42. Neil MacFarquhar, "Inside the Russian Troll Factory: Zombies and a Breakneck Pace," *New York Times*, February 18, 2017, https://www.nytimes.com/2018/02/18/world/europe/russia-troll-factory.html.
43. "One Professional Troll Tells All."
44. Christopher Paul and Miriam Mathews, "The Russian 'Firehose of Falsehood' Propaganda Model," RAND Corporation *Perspective*, 2016, https://www.rand.org/pubs/perspectives/PE198.html.
45. Ibid.
46. Ibidem.
47. Katy Zavadski, "Putin's Propaganda TV Lies about its Popularity," *The Daily Beast*, September 17, 2015, https://www.thedailybeast.com/putins-propaganda-tv-lies-about-its-popularity.
48. "Putin's Asymmetric Assault on Democracy in Russia And Europe: Implications for U.S. National Security," 41.
49. Jack Stubbs and Ginger Gleason, "Russia's RT America Registers as 'Foreign Agent' in U.S.," Reuters, November 13, 2017, https://www.reuters.com/article/us-russia-usa-media-restrictions-rt/russias-rt-america-registers-as-foreign-agent-in-u-s-idUSKBN1DD25B.
50. Holly Watt, "Ofcom Investigates Alex Salmond's TV Show on Kremlin-Backed Channel," *Guardian* (London), December 1, 2017, https://www.theguardian.com/world/2017/dec/18/ofcom-investigates-alex-salmonds-tv-show-kremlin-backed-network.
51. Dowling, "24-hour Putin People."
52. Zavadsky, "Putin's Propaganda TV Lies about Its Popularity."
53. Ibid.
54. "Putin's Asymmetric Assault on Democracy in Russia And Europe: Implications for U.S. National Security," 43.
55. Giles, "Russia's 'New' Tools for Confronting the West," 46.
56. Alina Polyakova, "The Next Russian Attack Will be Far Worse than Bots and Trolls," The Brookings Institution, March 22, 2018, https://www.brookings.edu/blog/order-from-chaos/2018/03/22/the-next-russian-attack-will-be-far-worse-than-bots-and-trolls.
57. Ibid.
58. Ibidem.
59. Ibidem.

60. Daisuke Wakabayashi and Nicholas Confessore, "Russia's Favored Outlet Is an Online News Giant. Youtube Helped," *New York Times*, October 23, 2017, https://www.nytimes.com/2017/10/23/technology/youtube-russia-rt.html.

61. "Deepfakes porn has serious consequences," BBC, February 3, 2018, http://www.bbc.com/news/technology-42912529.

62. Polyakova, "The Next Russian Attack Will Be Far Worse than Bots and Trolls."

63. Peter B. Doran and Donald N. Jensen, "Putin's Strategy of Chaos," *The American Interest*, March 1, 2018, https://www.the-american-interest.com/v/donald-n-jensen/.

64. Ibid.

CHINA SHAPES THE INTERNATIONAL MEDIA ENVIRONMENT

Peter Mattis and Samantha Hoffman

China's global rise has been accompanied by a growth in its capa-bilities to shape the international media environment and the way in which China is discussed internationally. Beijing's efforts to guide foreign opin-ion and shape its narratives are not the result of soft power, which the scholar Joseph Nye originally described as both passive and attractive. Rather, the Chinese Communist Party (CCP) has actively sought to ma-nipulate foreign perspectives on how China is understood. The CCP's ef-fort results from a wide-ranging of national security that sees those ideas that undermine the party's legitimacy and governance as threats. This understanding of security pushes the party toward preempting perceived threats and influencing the thinking of those who influence the foreign policy of other countries.

Although the CCP has not deployed sophisticated capabilities to manipulate social media or automate engagement on social media, the party nevertheless is successful using the traditional means of propagan-da to shape China-related narratives. The CCP influences democratic dis-course about China, but Beijing also makes many democratic states com-plicit in its intimidation of overseas Chinese and dissident communities.

The mistake many Westerners make in understanding the effec-tiveness of propaganda is a result of disproportionately focusing on the message itself, rather than the medium and means of transmission. This is particularly true in the case of China. Even if CCP messaging itself is not effective, its ability to control the media through which people engage and learn about China outside the country's borders signals three import-ant things. First, that the party's presence is ubiquitous, and borders are meaningless for those who wish to escape the CCP's influence. Second, that challenging the party, even outside China, is futile. The symbols of the party's presence – e.g., CCP-sponsored articles in government media outlets and propaganda inserts in Western papers – show that foreigners are lining up behind the party or tacitly support its rule. Third, and related, is when these messages are broadcast back into China, they convey the image that democratic governments stand behind the party, and therefore, the Chinese people are on their own and will receive no succor from the world's democracies.

Thus, responding to the CCP's propaganda challenge requires thinking about the medium more than the message. The party's approach has not necessarily promulgated persuasive messages, but it has squeezed the available space, especially in Chinese-language media, limiting the discourse of precisely the people with the cultural fluency to push back against the CCP's totalitarian principles and governance. Effective responses would reopen the public space for discussion of Chinese affairs, while removing the intimidating symbols that CCP control of the messaging media displays.

Here, a note on scope is necessary. This study analyzes Beijing's efforts to participate in and shape the international media environment. China's external propaganda efforts are far broader than just traditional media, and include a range of other activities like cultural and public diplomacy as well as "united front" work. The party departments and the central government ministries involved in this effort reflect this breadth. The party's Propaganda Department oversees traditional media operations both at home and abroad, but the United Front Work Department, Ministry of Education, Ministry of Culture, and the Ministry of Foreign Affairs all contribute to the effort.[1] Thus, although the CCP effort to use traditional media to influence those outside China is substantial, it only offers one, albeit important, part of the story.

THE VIEW FROM BEIJING

Accurately assessing what China is doing in the media environment both domestically and internationally requires first understanding how the party conceives of security. The PRC's concept of security heavily emphasizes preemption. Internal security is not as simple as forcefully ending incidents of civil unrest, while external security is not limited to issues such as managing relations with the United States. Rather, internal and external security entail managing the CCP and its power – that is, protecting the CCP from being delegitimized. Security, therefore is focused on protecting the Party's own position in power, not that of the Chinese state absent the Party. In practice, this means the CCP's methodologies for managing security threats are not limited to enhancing the capabilities of the People's Armed Police and the People's Liberation Army. They are also heavily focused on security in the ideological realm.

The country's 2015 National (State) Security Law defines security in the following terms:

> National (State) security refers to the relative absence of international or domestic threats to the state's power to govern, sovereignty, unity and territorial integrity, the welfare of the people, sustainable economic and social development, and other major national interests, and the ability to ensure a continued state of security. National security efforts shall adhere to a comprehensive understanding of national security, make the security of the People their goal, political security their basis and economic security their foundation; make military, cultural and social security their safeguard... [2]

This definition of security calls for an absence of threats, not simply the party's ability to manage them. Security is focused heavily on crisis prevention. As Xi Jinping noted: "We must put the prevention of risks in a prominent position. [We must] nip [risks] in the bud, and be concerned about what has yet to come to pass."[3] Failure to effectively prevent threats could mean that in the event of a crisis of legitimacy, the Party has already lost before any physical battle actually begins. Ideas do not shift a narrative overnight; narrative control is required far in advance of a conflict in order to have informational superiority.

The Party's primary process for "prevention of risks" is described in the Party's own language as "social management" (社会管理), or more euphemistically but with the exact same definition "social governance" (社会治理). Social management is a process best visualized as a cycle of Party-led shaping, managing and responding. It is a way of organization according to the Maoist "Mass Line" ideological mobilization methodology. Mao Zedong described the "mass line" as the process of the Communist Party taking the "scattered and unsystematic ideas of the masses," and forming them into "concentrated and systematic ideas," then taking them back to the masses to "propagate and explain these ideas until the masses embrace them as their own."[4] To achieve stability requires the successful management of problems so they do not develop beyond the Party's capacity for control. The process of shaping, managing and responding must be automatic. The concept of social management is embedded in almost everything, because to the CCP everything is linked to politics and security.

Since state security is largely focused on security in the ideological realm, the process for ensuring it does not stop at China's borders, even if it takes a slightly different form beyond them. Outside of China, social management is embedded in official thinking about, and approaches to, the concept of global governance. In global governance, social management is largely about shaping the direction of international conversations – often expressed in shaping discussion of subjects ranging from sovereignty to cyberspace security in ways that accommodate the CCP's viewpoints. Thus, the role of media, in the official Chinese conception, is to avoid discussion of issues and themes the PRC perceives as threatening, while simultaneously promoting discussion that favors CCP viewpoints, and which can eventually drown out those unfavorable to the CCP. This helps to explain why Xi Jinping, during his well-publicized visits to the *People's Daily*, CCTV, and Xinhua, made clear that: "the mission of the Party's media work is to provide guidance for the public, serve the country's overall interests, unite the general public, instill confidence and pool strength, tell right from wrong and connect China to the world."[5]

The CCP has the objective of achieving "discourse power" or "right to speak" (话语权). The concept of discourse power "is an extension of soft power, relating to influence and attractiveness of a country's ideology and value system."[6] One of the greatest threats the PRC perceives in relation to protecting the party in the ideological realm is that "hostile forces," either domestic or foreign, attempt to subvert China through ideas. For instance, the CCP concluded that the Color Revolutions that took place throughout the "post-Soviet space" in the early 2000s were driven by "raging domestic grievances, electoral politics exploited by the opposition, and Western powers' (the United States in particular) intervention for geo-strategic interests."[7] While this may not be entirely true, it does not matter. Rather, it reflects the CCP's longstanding perception that hostile external actors, like the U.S., meddle in the "internal affairs" of other countries and are, therefore, a threat.

This thinking dates back to the Cold War, but today such fears are amplified by the spread of information and proliferation of technology. The resulting information insecurity was seen as a key factor in delegitimizing the governments affected by the Color Revolutions. Thus Chinese authorities have come to view the free flow of information as a threat – or, as the "Document No. 9," promulgated in Spring 2013, puts it, Western journalism "undermine[s] our country's principle that the media should be infused with the spirit of the Party."[8]

Indeed, the party places cultural security and social security on a par with the military in terms of priorities to protect the Chinese system. Cultural security requires promoting core socialist values, and preventing infiltration or sabotage by outside cultures, particularly western democracies. Cultural power is a key source of sustainable national power. As one article in the official *Beijing Daily* explained, "The discourse power must focus on the 'discourse,'" and "over the course of China's revolution, development and reform, it has persistently put emphasis on ethnic characteristics such as literature and art, culture, and ideology."[9] It is also why, as Chinese authorities see it, media falls in the realm of information security, which is required for ensuring social security through the management of public opinion.

A TIGHTENING DOMESTIC NOOSE

China's media environment has consistently ranked as "Not Free," owing to the substantial tools brought to bear by the party in order to control public expression. As Freedom House's *Freedom of the Press 2017* report concluded, "The ruling CCP maintains control over news reporting via direct ownership, accreditation of journalists, harsh penalties for online criticism, and daily directives to media outlets and websites that guide coverage of breaking news stories."[10] The restrictive environment that prevails today is the product of roughly 15 years of the CCP steadily constricting the space available for independent and investigative journalism within China. Although the domestic media environment is undoubtedly more diverse and open than in the days of Mao Zedong and the early days of Deng Xiaoping's Reform and Opening, the CCP has re-exerted control over Chinese domestic media in order to ensure that even commercially-driven publications stay safely within the bounds of party guidance.

In the glory days of the 1990s, the profit motive of commercial spinoffs from party-owned outlets allowed journalists to exploit the gaps in public opinion guidance to produce investigative reporting that exposed abuses and pushed the boundaries of censorship. The Internet also allowed local stories to go national in ways previously unappreciated by the party leadership. But beginning in 2003, that began to change. Coverage of the SARS outbreak and the proliferation of stories of official abuse led party officials to conclude that commercially-driven media was challenging the party's guidance of public opinion, and that the party needed to respond. Directives became more frequent and specific. Prohibitions on cross-regional reporting were put in place. In 2005, the Propaganda Department, including its provincial departments and local bureaus, began placing cadres directly inside publications to shape their reporting from the inside. In early 2013, the overbearing nature of these propaganda cadres came to a head over a New Year's editorial at the *Southern Weekly*, leading to protests in Guangzhou and Ningbo. These "freedom of the press" protests were more a call for a return to the more open (but still censored) days of the 1990s than the unreasonable hope that the CCP would end censorship.[11] For this brief moment following the 18th Party Congress and Xi Jinping's ascension to power, observers had hope that Beijing's censorship regime and public opinion guidance might be relaxed.

But the opposite happened. Xi Jinping's tenure has seen China's media environment become increasingly restrictive. China's new leader made it clear that news must serve the party's needs, and explicitly legislated a proactive responsibility to protect the party-state. In the spring of 2013, the CCP promulgated the aforementioned "Document No. 9," placing an official policy stamp on views long held within the party about the danger to national security of Western-style freedom of the press. The rest of Xi's views on media would become clear in February 2016, when he visited the *People's Daily*, China Central Television, and the Xinhua News Agency. The *People's Daily* article relaying Xi's speech on the media stressed the official view that "All work of the Party's news and public opinion media must reflect the will of the Party ... preserve the authority of the Party, preserve the unity of the Party, and achieve love of the Party ... maintaining a high level of uniformity with the Party in ideology, politics and action."[12]

This effort is backed by a broad range of legislation on state security, including: the Counter-Espionage Law (2014); the State Security Law (2015); the Foreign Non-Governmental Organization Management Law (2016); the Cyber Security Law (2016); and, the Intelligence Law (2017). Each piece of legislation focuses heavily on the concept of individual "responsibility" to the Party. For instance, article 11 of the State Security Law (2015) clearly states that "Citizens of the People's Republic of China, every state organ and the armed forces, each political party, the militia, enterprises, public institutions and social organizations, all have the responsibility and obligation to maintain state security."[13]

Individual "responsibility" to uphold the Party is not a new concept particular to Xi. In fact, it can be found in Mao-era political mobilization strategies. If the concept ever diminished in importance, it clearly re-appeared following the 1989 Tiananmen massacre, when "responsibility" became strongly linked to "social management."[14] The recent emphasis on individual responsibility in the law is tied directly to the "discourse power" concept, and the campaign under Xi Jinping to silence critics.

This effort began very early in Xi's tenure, notably with the silencing of Sina Weibo's so-called "Big V" high-profile users, who were often critical of the government and had the platform to influence millions.[15] One of the Big V, Chinese-American entrepreneur Charles Xue (also known as Xue Manzi), was detained for eight months on charges of seeking prostitutes, and later released on bail in April 2014. Xue, who had already "confessed" to his crimes on Chinese state television, subsequently posted on his Weibo account: "Through my lack of self-discipline and mistakes, I've brought irreparable harm to my family, and for this I apologize sincerely to my wife and family members... At the same time, I bow earnestly and sincerely in the direction of my followers. I'm sorry. The old man disappointed you."[16] Another, Qin Zhihui, was found guilty of "slander" and of "picking quarrels and provoking troubles," and sentenced to three years in prison.

The Cyberspace Administration of China (CAC), a branch of the CCP Propaganda Department, is responsible for enforcing these rules in the online environment. In 2017, the CAC passed regulations inserting the party into the distribution of news online as well as determining what news could be produced. Pursuant to the ordinance, from June 1, 2017, all political, economic, military, or diplomatic reports or opinion articles on blogs, websites, forums, search engines, instant messaging apps and all other platforms that select or edit news and information would need to have party-approved editorial staff.[17] Since that time, the CAC has strengthened enforcement of online content with support of the Cyber Security Law (2016). In August 2017, three leading social media platforms, Sina Weibo, Tencent's WeChat and Baidu's Tieba, were all put under investigation for spreading terrorism, false rumors and obscene content deemed a "threat to state security, public safety and social order."[18]

CHINA'S TOOLS OF INTERNATIONAL INFLUENCE

The CCP Propaganda Department has long deployed internationally-oriented media to spread the party's message, but its instruments of influence have expanded significantly in recent years.

CCTV's international arm became China Global Television Network (CGTN) in December 2016 as part of an effort to rebrand the party's international broadcasting.[19] CGTN, according to its website, boasts reporting teams in 70 countries, a 24-hour English-language news service, and also broadcasts in Spanish, French, Arabic, and Russian. Television broadcasts are supplemented by a robust digital presence across Chinese and international social media platforms, including those banned inside China. The station hires experienced local journalists.[20]

China Radio International (CRI) was created on December 3, 1941 as the Xinhua Radio Station to broadcast CCP propaganda across China. Today, CRI claims to broadcast in 65 languages from 101 radio stations reaching across 50 countries with 3,000 hours of programming daily.[21] The English-language service began in 1947, and today includes 400 hours of programming on radio, video, and mobile app platforms. CRI also partners with local radio stations in China's border provinces – Inner Mongolia, Jilin, Heilongjiang, and Yunnan – to provide targeted content for neighboring countries. In the last 15 years, two dates stand out in Beijing's outward propaganda as it relates to CRI. First, in 2006, CRI established its first overseas stations in Kenya and Laos. Second, in 2011, CRI expanded beyond radio to include Internet television and radio as well mobile apps for streaming audio and video programming.[22]

At the most recent National People's Congress in March 2018, Beijing announced plans to merge CCTV with CRI and China National Radio into the "Voice of China." The English-language version of the *People's Daily* explained the organizational restructuring explicitly in national security terms, because of "the need for a 'super voice' to drown out the anti-China propaganda" and to "ensure its voice is heard loud and clear around the world."[23] The full implications of this organizational shift have not yet become clear, but presumably the "Voice of China" will provide more integrated news production across the different outlets.

Finally, Beijing puts out several English-language publications, including the *China Daily* and translations of selected Xinhua, *People's Daily*, and *Global Times* articles. The *China Daily* provides, according to its website, "a voice of China on the global stage." Founded in 1981, the paper now has a daily circulation of 900,000 copies printed from 34 sites overseas.[24] The paper can be found internationally in airport lounges, hotels, newspaper stands, and anywhere else newspapers can be found. Unlike its translated counterparts, the *China Daily* contains content designed to appeal to foreigners about Chinese culture and positive stories of Chinese economic and political developments. The other three outlets provide basic information about official activities, as well as editorial comments on issues important to Beijing.

In addition to these flagship media organizations, Beijing has adopted at least two other measures in order to extend its reach internationally. The first is the acquisition or indirect control through proxies of overseas Chinese-language media outlets. The full scope of this activity worldwide has not been gauged, but it is estimated to be extensive. For example, one Chinese newspaper editor suggested that as much as 95 percent of the Chinese-language media in Australia is owned by the CCP or its proxies.[25] Similarly, a 2015 Reuters investigation uncovered that 33 radio stations in 14 countries were run by CRI.[26] The party was able to pressure such outlets to sell out or concede their autonomy by targeting their advertising revenue. Companies that advertise with independent or Falun Gong media might be directly pressured by officials from the Chinese embassy or consulate. If a company has an office in China, security officials may visit the office to deliver the message in person.[27]

The second method is compromising private and public media platforms as well as media personalities in foreign countries. In the case of the Australian Broadcast Corporation (ABC), the company signed an agreement with the CCP Propaganda Department and began censoring its Chinese-language broadcasting to increase revenues and its ostensible reach into China.[28] CRI likewise worked out agreements with the Associated Press and Reuters, but the details and impact of these deals cannot be discerned from public sources.[29] China's intelligence services also have devoted time to cultivating and recruiting agents among journalists working for government-sponsored Chinese-language broadcast services. This gives Beijing a direct hand in shaping the careers of journalists and how China is covered. In Taiwan, anyone with a media platform – be they journalist, pundit, scholar, or celebrity – is a potential target for recruitment. Because this relationship does not involve the compromise of government secrets, democratic governments often have trouble addressing the problem.[30]

One element notably absent in China's external propaganda strategy is the aggressive Russian-style manipulation of social media to stoke resentment and discredit targeted political systems. The only arena in which such activity is beginning to emerge is Taiwan. Last summer, Taiwan's National Security Council publicized suspected Chinese activity on social media, including content farms that tried to skew social media conversations and exaggerate disturbances.[31] As such, Taiwan warrants monitoring and may represent peak Chinese propaganda capabilities. However, such tactics do not appear to have been deployed against the rest of the world.

THE EFFECTIVENESS OF CHINESE PROPAGANDA

The conventional wisdom about CCP propaganda abroad is that it cannot work to create soft power. Success faces two significant obstacles. The first is that propaganda only works at home because of the coercion behind it, since Chinese people largely ignore the visible signs around them. The second is the contradiction between the party's requirement for political correctness and the need to be persuasive for a global audience. As Hilton Yip has written in *Foreign Policy*, "The redoubling of efforts to push the party's theories and principles abroad is at odds with boosting China's overseas image... As long as China's leadership cannot differentiate between propaganda and journalism, the Voice of China will stay unheard."[32] This logic only makes sense if one confines propaganda to the bare content of the message, rather than ownership of the medium. But even the China-related narratives used in Western media sometimes bear the hallmarks of the party's propaganda.

Among the most noticeable of the CCP's narratives that have found a place in Western media and public conversations relate to the Chinese people's relationship to the party, China's rise, and tensions in the Taiwan Strait. The CCP claims to represent all Chinese people, regardless of their citizenship or where they live.[33] Although the most egregious abuses – such as the seemingly arbitrary arrest of overseas Chinese with foreign citizenship – rightly earn censure, foreign analysts and officials nevertheless often fall into the trap of agreeing with the party. One of the most notable recent examples was FBI Director Christopher Wray's characteristic of Chinese espionage and influence as a "whole-of-society" effort, a description that garnered protests from Asian-American groups.[34] Repeating the party line has practical consequences. Because Wray did not distinguish between the party's policies and how Chinese people, including PRC citizens and overseas Chinese with foreign citizenship, actually respond, he inflated his identified adversary's supposed strength and reinforced misconceptions of a monolithic, CCP-led China. Both problems fly in the face of the party's actual rule of China, which is marred by contention between Chinese society and the party state as well as factional infighting within the party itself. They also reinforce the narrative, propounded by the CCP, of the futility of opposing China's rise.

The CCP has consistently attempted to paint China's rise as an inevitable consequence of the party's policies and wise leadership. Non-Chinese elites, in turn, pick up on these ideas in their writings and speeches, placing them in august forums and standard-bearing newspapers.[35] Those who express concern or hope for China's political decay and collapse receive vituperative attacks from CCP-controlled media outlets and proxies – attacks that describe them as "frivolous," having "lost their minds," and individuals whose "obsession with this illusion has deprived them of rational and critical thinking."[36] Relatedly, media and foreign analysts also regularly use the CCP's term "anti-China" to describe skeptics or those who favor dealing with China on a more reciprocal footing. Despite the best efforts of some of those critics to focus on the party itself, "anti-China" is used as a way to discredit their views and, at times, insinuate racism motivates their charges against the CCP – a natural result of the conflation between party and people.[37]

Last but not least, foreign media organizations regularly refer to cross-strait tensions between China and Taiwan as agent-less phenomena, rather than the result of Beijing's objectives and actions. As long-time Taiwan resident and observer Michael Turton has observed, "the ideological construct [is] that China-Taiwan relations are a site of tensions driven by Taiwan's actions, to which China reacts without any agency of its own, as if its reactions are involuntary reflexes rather than policy choices."[38] Implicit in this construct is the view that low cross-strait tensions are good, and that the way to resolve them is for Taiwan to be less provocative. Taiwan, however, is not threatening to declare *de jure* independence, nor is its government anti-China.

In addition to successfully injecting several narratives into the way foreigners frame China-related issues, the CCP has effectively squeezed out alternative Chinese-language voices abroad. The largest network of non-CCP media outlets, both newspapers and radio, are supported by the Falun Gong. They survive because they have independent financial support and are not as dependent on advertising as are independent outlets. For both reasonable reasons, such as occasionally exaggerated reporting, and unreasonable ones (such as being a group that the CCP persecutes) Falun Gong media lacks credibility beyond the comparatively small circle of practitioners and experienced, well-informed readers who can sift out problematic reporting. Apart from the Falun Gong, the other significant alternative source of Chinese-language news comes from government broadcasters. Yet, even these outlets have had persistent problems, as was outlined above.

Controlling the Chinese-language media sends an important signal about the party's reach to overseas Chinese and PRC citizens traveling abroad: the party is everywhere. In isolation, the Chinese-language media landscape might not be that imposing. In combination with the party's moves to co-opt Chinese community organizations and establish party cells abroad as well as intimidation, it contributes to the image of an unchallengeable party that cannot be escaped. Rather than reading local content about local concerns or other stories that matter, CCP-controlled media may reprint stories from Xinhua, the *People's Daily*, and other party mouthpieces back in China. It is control of the medium, not the content or the quality of the message, that creates the effect.

MORAL HAZARD

In many respects, the people of democratic states have become a version of Vaclav Havel's greengrocer who dutifully places the symbols of regime loyalty in his shop window.[39] The difference, obviously, is that democratic greengrocers rarely face the power of the Chinese party-state directly, and are less vulnerable to its coercion. These symbols of loyalty do little for anyone who does not deal with China, and their symbolism may not even be understood by those who display them. Although this problem has some overlap with the acceptance of CCP narratives and ways of speaking, the symbols of the party displayed outside China go beyond words. Such symbols include the China Watch supplements placed in foreign papers as paid advertisements, and the presence of *China Daily* newspapers in shops and on the streets, especially in the absence of alternative Chinese voices.

As Vaclav Havel pointed out, the problem with these symbols is not that people believe in them, but that they display the ubiquitous and intimidating presence of the state. So, too, with contemporary Chinese propaganda; it is not that democratic societies necessarily approve of what the CCP says or of how it maintains power – they likely do not – but that their acceptance and promotion of Chinese narratives conveys an acceptance of the permanence and reach of the party itself.

In China, CCP slogans appear on billboards, neatly-shaped hedgerows, the sides of buildings, banners, and any other place a Westerner might be accustomed to seeing commercial advertising. Whether the signage displays "core consciousness," the "China Dream," or the "four comprehensives" is largely irrelevant, because the significance lies in the medium rather than the message.[40] These displays show the party's presence in everyday life and the futility of opposing it. Similarly, many of the people who exhibit CCP symbols may not be aware of their meaning. However, those who deal with China or are Chinese understand it very well, and these are precisely the people who possess the knowledge and cultural fluency to undermine the CCP's power. These symbols send a message to Chinese traveling abroad or diaspora communities that democratic governments are indifferent to the CCP's reach, and reinforce the encompassing nature and reach of the party.

The purpose and effectiveness of CCP propaganda cannot be understood simply by looking at the messages or their persuasiveness to foreigners. Propaganda should be understood as a method of control, particularly by removing the public space for perspectives at odds with CCP narratives. The persistent presence of party propaganda signals to overseas Chinese and cognizant outsiders that the CCP has successfully gained a foothold that will not be easily dislodged. If democratic institutions willingly display the narratives, language, and symbols of totalitarian control, then those same institutions also waver in their commitment to democratic values.

Addressing the challenges of Beijing's international propaganda campaign will require a threefold approach. First, care must be taken to remove the willingness of democratic institutions to display the symbols of CCP propaganda. Rather than being unwitting greengrocers, citizens of democratic states need to be more cognizant of what Chinese narratives, publications, and symbols they pick up and promote. Second, democratic states should increase state funding and opportunities for independent Chinese-language media in print and on air. These media organizations need to be protected, because of the CCP's persistent efforts to undermine, discredit, and/or manipulate them. Doing so will ensure there is always an alternative voice with integrity available to Chinese media consumers.

Finally, the CCP's intimidation of independent media organizations should not be tolerated, and pushback given where possible. If intimidation is carried out by embassy and consular officials, then demarches and possibly even expulsion for activities violating diplomatic conventions should follow. Such measures should not be seen as being against China or the CCP. Rather, they would represent a forceful stand for democratic values, and a commitment to ensuring that the public space remains available for alternative views of the future of China that go beyond party narratives.

ENDNOTES

1. Anne-Marie Brady, "China's Foreign Propaganda Machine," *Journal of Democracy* 26, no. 4, October 2015, 51-59; Peter Mattis, "An American Lens on Chinese Interference and Influence-Building Abroad," *Asan Forum*, April 30, 2018, http://www.theasanforum. org/an-american-lens-on-chinas-interference-and-influence-building-abroad/.

2. 中华人民共和国国家安全法 (State Security Law of the People's Republic of China), July 2015, http://www.npc.gov.cn/npc/xinwen/2015-07/07/content_1941161.htm.

3. "指导新时代国家安全工作的强大思想武器—学习《习近平关于总体国家安全观论述摘编 (A Powerful Ideological Weapon for Guiding National Security in a New Era – Learn from *Excerpts of Xi Jinping's Discussions Related to the Comprehensive National Security Concept*)," *People's Daily*, May 4, 2018, http://politics. people.com.cn/n1/2018/0504/c1001-29963982.html.

4. Timothy Heath, "Xi's Mass Line Campaign: Realigning Party Politics to New Realities," Jamestown Foundation *China Brief* 13, no. 16, August 9, 2013, https://jamestown.org/program/xis-mass-line-campaign-realigning-party-politics-to-new-realities/; Mao Zedong, "Some Questions Concerning Methods of Leadership ," June 1, 1943, as reprinted on https://www.marxists.org/reference/archive/mao/selected-works/volume-3/mswv3_13.htm.

5. "News Organizations Should Better Serve the People: Xinhua President," Xinhua, February 19, 2018. http://www.xinhuanet.com/english/2018-02/19/c_136985413.htm.

6. Mattis, "An American Lens on China's Interference and Influence-Building Abroad"; See also Peter Mattis, "China's International Right to Speak," Jamestown Foundation *China Brief* 12, no. 20, October 19, 2012, https://jamestown.org/program/chinas-international-right-to-speak/.

7. Titus C. Chen, "China's Reaction to the Color Revolutions: Adaptive Authoritarianism in Full Swing," *Asian Perspective* 34, no. 2, 2010, 1-2.

8. "Document 9: A ChinaFile Translation," *ChinaFile*, November 8, 2013, http://www.chinafile.com/document-9-chinafile-translation.

9. Wenzhao Tao, "从国情与发展趋势看，既要重视 "独善其身"

的中国特色，又要有"兼济天下"的世界情怀—"穷"与"达"：中国话语权的辩证法 (From the Perspective of the State, the Country and Developmental Trends, We Must Maintain the Chinese Characteristic of 'Attend to One's Own Virtue in Solitude,' while Possessing the Passion to 'Extend Virtue to All Under the Heavens' – Being 'Poor' and 'Well-Off'; a Dialectic on Chinese Discourse Power)," *Beijing Daily*, January 14, 2017, http://opinion.zjol.com.cn/rdht/201701/t20170114_2830487.shtml.

10. Freedom House, "Freedom of the Press 2017: China," 2017, https://freedomhouse.org/report/freedom-press/2017/china.

11. David Bandurski, "How the Southern Weekly Protests Moved the Bar on Press Control," Jamestown Foundation *China Brief* 13, iss. 3, February 1, 2013, https://jamestown.org/program/how-the-southern-weekly-protests-moved-the-bar-on-press-control/.

12. "坚持正确方向创新方法手段 提高新闻舆论传播力引导力 (Adhere to the Right Direction, Innovate the Methods and Means to Strengthen Broadcasting and Guiding the News and Public Opinion)," Xinhua, February 19, 2016, http://politics.people.com.cn/n1/2016/0219/c1024-28136159.html.

13. State Security Law of the People's Republic of China.

14. See Samantha Hoffman, "Programming China: The Communist Party's Autonomic Approach to Managing State Security," Ph.D. Dissertation, The University of Nottingham, September 29, 2017.

15. "微博"大V"话语权边界及其有效行使 (The Boundaries and Effectives of 'Big V' Weibo Accounts)," People's Net, July 11, 2017, http://media.people.com.cn/n1/2017/0711/c413303-29397007.html.

16. Josh Chin, "Out on Bail, Chinese Social Media Star Xue Manzi Returns to Weibo," *Wall Street Journal*, April 19, 2014. https://blogs.wsj.com/chinarealtime/2014/04/19/u-s-venture-capitalist-xue-apolgizes-in-china-for-alleged-transgressions/.

17. Christian Sheperd and Robert Birsel, "China tightens rules on online news, network providers," Reuters, May 2, 2017. https://www.reuters.com/article/us-china-internet-censorship-security/china-tightens-rules-on-online-news-network-providers-idUSKBN17Y0Y6?feedType=RSS&feedName=worldNews.

18. "腾讯微信、新浪微博、百度贴吧被立案调查 (Tencent's WeChat, Sina Weibo and Baidu Tieba Under Investigation)," Xinhua, August 11, 2017, http://www.xinhuanet.com/fortune/2017-08/11/c_1121468759.htm.

19. "China's state broadcaster CCTV rebrands international networks as CGTN in global push," Associated Press, December 31, 2016. http://www.scmp.com/news/china/policies-politics/article/2058429/chinas-state-broadcaster-cctv-rebrands-international.

20. For example, CGTN America hired a diverse set of anchors and journalists, including award winning journalists and media entrepreneurs. See CGTN America, "Anchors and Correspondents," n.d., https://america.cgtn.com/anchors-corresp.

21. China Radio International, "关于CRI - 中国国际广播电台 (About CRI - China Radio International)," n.d., http://www.cri.com.cn/about.

22. China Radio International, "History - China Plus," February 16, 2017, http://chinaplus.cri.cn/aboutus/aboutcri/62/20170216/391.html.

23. Curtis Stone, "World needs a better understanding of China, 'Voice of China' can help," *People's Daily*, March 22, 2018, http://en.people.cn/n3/2018/0322/c90000-9440715.html.

24. China Daily, "About China Daily Group," n.d., http://www.chinadaily.com.cn/static_e/aboutus.html.

25. Kelsey Munro and Philip Wen, "Chinese language newspapers in Australia: Beijing controls messaging, propaganda in press," *Sydney Morning Herald*, July 8, 2016, https://www.smh.com.au/national/chinese-language-newspapers-in-australia-beijing-controls-messaging-propaganda-in-press-20160610-gpg0s3.html.

26. Koh Gui Qing and John Shiffman, "Beijing's covert radio network airs China-friendly news across Washington, and the world," Reuters, November 2, 2015, https://www.reuters.com/investigates/special-report/china-radio/.

27. Tara Francis Chan, "One chilling story shows how far China will go to silence critics," *Business Insider*, May 2, 2018, https://www.businessinsider.sg/chinese-influence-in-australia-media-2018-5/?r=US&IR=T.

28. "ABC and the Great Firewall of China," *ABC Media Watch*, May 9, 2016, http://www.abc.net.au/mediawatch/transcripts/s4458872.htm.

29. China Radio International, "What We Do - China Plus," February 16, 2017, http://chinaplus.cri.cn/aboutus/aboutcri/62/20170216/392.html.

30. Interviews by Peter Mattis, Taipei, Taiwan, July 2017.

31. Peter Mattis, "Counterintelligence Remains Weakness in Taiwan's Defense," Jamestown Foundation *China Brief* 17, iss. 11, August 17, 2017, https://jamestown.org/program/counterintelligence-remains-weakness-in-taiwans-defense/.

32. Hilton Yip, "China's $6 Billion Propaganda Blitz Is a Snooze," *Foreign Policy*, April 23, 2018, http://foreignpolicy.com/2018/04/23/the-voice-of-china-will-be-a-squeak/.

33. For example, "说说陕西海外华人华侨的心声 (Talk About the Aspirations of Overseas Chinese and Ethnic Chinese from Shaanxi Province)," Shaanxi People's Political Consultative Conference General Office, http://www.sxzx.gov.cn/zxhy/p/12146.html; Yang Zhu, and Chen Tian. "华侨华人对中国未来充满信心 (Overseas Chinese and Ethnic Chinese Express Full Confidence in China's Future)," *People's Daily*, October 30, 2017, http://paper.people.com.cn/rmrbhwb/html/2017-10/30/content_1813264.htm; "仰望伟大的中华民族 (Looking Up at the Great Chinese Nation)," *People's Daily*, April 24, 2018, http://wmzh.china.com.cn/2018-04/24/content_40304186.htm.

34. Betsy Woodruff and Julia Arciga, "FBI Director's Shock Claim: Chinese Students Are a Potential Threat," *The Daily Beast*, February 13, 2018, https://www.thedailybeast.com/fbi-directors-shock-claim-chinese-students-are-a-potential-threat.

35. For example, Lawrence Summers, "Grasp the Reality of China's Rise," *Financial Times*, November 9, 2015, https://www.ft.com/content/284b68f8-84ab-11e5-8e80-1574112844fd; Arvind Subramanian, "The Inevitable Superpower: Why China's Dominance is a Sure Thing," *Foreign Affairs*, September/October 2011, https://www.foreignaffairs.com/articles/china/2011-08-19/inevitable-superpower.

36. "West's Bigotry Causes China Collapse Fantasy," *Global Times*, March 4, 2015, http://www.globaltimes.cn/content/910050.shtml.

37. For example, Bob Carr, "Australia's anti-China stance is a misguided attempt to cozy up to Trump," *South China Morning Post*, February 19, 2018, http://www.scmp.com/comment/insight-opinion/article/2133792/australias-anti-china-stance-misguided-attempt-cosy-trump. For a description of how this logic unfolds, see Alex Joske, "Framing the Australia-China Relationship," ASPI *Strategist*, April 24, 2018, https://www.aspistrategist.org.au/framing-australia-china-relationship/.

38. Michael Turton, "Exploiting Cross-Strait Tensions for Fun and Profit," *The News Lens*, April 10, 2018, https://international.thenewslens.com/article/93238.

39. The greengrocer analogy appears in Vaclav Havel's famous October 1978 essay, "The Power of the Powerless." It was subsequently republished in Vaclav Havel et al., *The Power of the Powerless: Citizens Against the State in Central Eastern Europe* (Routledge, 1985).

40. One party official admitted to the authors that she did not even notice the prevalence of propaganda slogans visibly displayed in public, observing it might because she was so accustomed to their presence.

THE ISLAMIST TAKEOVER OF TURKISH MEDIA
Aykan Erdemir and Merve Tahiroglu

When Turkey's Islamist-rooted Justice and Development Party (AKP) came to power with 34 percent of the vote in the 2002 elections, its media outreach was largely restricted to a small fringe group of Islamist outlets. But in the decade-and-a-half since his ascent to power, AKP leader Recep Tayyip Erdoğan has come to control nearly the entirety of Turkey's media, either through ownership or intimidation. Not only has the AKP transformed Turkey's state-owned media organs into partisan outlets, but Erdoğan's family members and business cronies have come to control seven key media conglomerates[1] that now own 21 of Turkey's 29 dailies, effectively capturing 90 percent of national circulation.[2]

Erdoğan's colonization and weaponization of the Turkish media has taken over twenty years, and picked up speed following the abortive coup of July 2016. Using emergency decrees, and under the pretext of combatting terrorism, Erdoğan shuttered 177 media outlets in the span of five months in the second half of 2016.[3] Under Erdoğan's rule, Turkey has imprisoned 535 members of the press,[4] in the process becoming the world's top jailer of journalists.[5] In turn, the systematic harassment and intimidation of remaining journalists and media outlets has led to widespread self-censorship, further hindering critical reporting.

Erdoğan pursues both domestic and international goals in building and weaponizing a media empire. At home, the Turkish president uses the media to defame adversaries, consolidate his one-man regime, and further Islamist social engineering. Globally, the media has become a key tool for providing legitimacy to the AKP, especially during its early years, by portraying the Islamist party as a moderate "Muslim democrat" faction modeled after Europe's Christian democratic parties. Following Erdoğan's consolidation of power, however, the AKP's transnational Islamist agenda and its challenge to the Western liberal world order became more pronounced, and is advanced in particular through the multi-lingual editions of the state-owned *TRT* and Anadolu Agency, as well as the pro-government English-language newspaper *Daily Sabah*.

In today's Turkey, a handful of independent dailies, such as *BirGün*, *Cumhuriyet*, *Evrensel*, *Sözcü*, and *Yurt*, and the weeklies *Agos* and *Şalom*, continue to struggle, against great odds, to provide critical coverage to their readers. Many citizens have turned to online outlets like *Bianet*, *Diken*, *Duvar*, *Haberdar*, *Sendika.Org*, and *T24* for alternative news. On Turkey's leading satellite television provider, only one opposition TV channel (*Halk TV*) remains; Erdoğan has come to dominate the entire broadcasting industry.

Today, Turkey's president feels he has won the battle against free media at home and uses his media empire to manufacture consent and mobilize the electorate to bolster his majoritarian regime. Consequently, he is turning his energies toward weaponizing the media for his global ambitions, and pointing it increasingly toward the West.

A HOSTILE TAKEOVER

Erdoğan and his acolytes built their media empire both by launching new media outlets and by acquiring existing ones through their conglomerates and a series of corrupt deals over the course of the AKP's 16-year-long rule. Throughout this period, Erdoğan worked systematically to dismantle outlets or channels that opposed his leadership, whether by shutting them down entirely or by demanding the sacking of individual journalists. This is the story of how Turkey's most prominent Islamists colonized the country's media.

Building and boosting Turkey's Islamist media
When the AKP came to power in 2002, the Turkish media scene was already characterized by what analyst Andrew Finkel refers to as "media capture"–whereby a handful of media bosses who "wanted to maximize [their] influence in non-press economic spheres" were coopted by political leaders with whom they entered into a "symbiotic but mutually corrupting relationship."[6] In addition to civilian special interests, the Turkish military also exerted substantial pressure on the media, going as far as fabricating evidence to frame critical journalists for support of terrorism, triggering mass layoffs and even carrying out physical attacks against members of the press.[7] Nevertheless, the existence of numerous

media conglomerates with competing interests led to a fragmented media landscape, and hence to polyvocality. Still, a number of taboo topics, such as the Kurdish question and military affairs, were for the most part off limits in the mainstream press.

Before the AKP's rise to power, Turkey's Islamists owned a few media outlets with a small audience, controlled largely by two strands of Islamic tradition: the Islamist politician Necmettin Erbakan's National Vision Movement, and cleric Fethullah Gülen's Hizmet Movement, better known in Turkey and abroad as the Gülen Movement. Turkey's dominant media conglomerates, for the most part, were critical of and even hostile to Islamist movements and politics. Erdoğan's ascendancy in national politics necessitated not only the bolstering of Turkey's Islamist media, but also the capture of existing media conglomerates and the construction of new ones.

From the 1970s until the founding of the AKP in 2001, Erdoğan worked for Erbakan's successive political parties, all of which were shut down for violating the Turkish Constitution's provisions concerning secularism. Erdoğan also allied with Gülen and his supporters to boost a common ideal of publicizing Islamist politics as compatible with democratic rule. While Erdoğan ultimately broke with both allies and carved his own path to the detriment of these groups, he used both movements' finances, human resources, and media to boost his and his party's popularity, both at home and abroad.

Turkey's first Islamist television channel, *Kanal 7*, for example, was established in 1994 on Erbakan's orders, and thanks to Erdogan's efforts. That year, Erdoğan was elected the mayor of Istanbul via Erbakan's Welfare Party, whose members concurrently founded *Kanal 7*. For the next three years, between 1994 and 1997, Erdoğan not only rented out his municipality's radio and television broadcasting infrastructure to *Kanal 7*, but also spent 20 percent of the municipality's advertising budget on the channel.[8]

Meanwhile, a corporation known as Albayrak Holding acquired the small Islamist daily *Yeni Şafak* from a like-minded NGO in 1997. Both the channel and the publication would benefit immensely from Erdoğan's political success in subsequent years; in September 2003, only months after the AKP's election to power, *Kanal 7*'s parent company nearly quadrupled its capital,[9] and in 2005, a key *Kanal 7* official was appointed as the president of Turkey's official broadcasting regulatory agency.[10]

Along with these two outlets, the daily *Yeni Şafak* and *Kanal 7*, the Erdoğan-allied Gülen movement's media companies served as the AKP's top public relations tool during the early 2000s. Of these, the Gülenist newspaper *Zaman*, which had been launched in 1986 by the Feza Media Group, became an AKP mouthpiece during the party's first decade in power.[11] In turn, *Zaman*'s audience proliferated across the world; by 2007, the newspaper had managed to launch editions in Australia, Azerbaijan, Russia's Bashkortostan region, Bulgaria, Canada, Cyprus, Germany, Romania, Kazakhstan, Kyrgyzstan, Macedonia, Russia's republic of Tatarstan, Turkmenistan, and the U.S.[12] Meanwhile the English-language daily *Today's Zaman* played a key role in legitimizing the AKP to Western audiences, presenting the party as Turkey's liberal reformists who had abandoned their Islamist past.

Acquiring Turkey's secular/independent media

But the AKP did not stop with Turkey's Islamist media. Through a series of shady deals, it promoted the sale of bankrupt media companies seized by the country's Savings Deposit Insurance Fund (TMSF) to Erdoğan's business cronies. These companies changed hands several times between pro-AKP moguls throughout the party's decade in power, but were all effectively converted from independent media outlets to the government's publicity organs. The former owners of these media outlets or groups were either forced to default on their businesses or prosecuted in sham trials on charges of coup plotting or terrorism. The government also silenced any investigation into corruption regarding the acquisitions. The main actors in this process were not only Erdoğan's son-in-law Berat Albayrak's Çalık Holding and the Gülen-affiliated Koza-İpek Group, but also other Turkish moguls like Ethem Sancak and Ömer Faruk Kalyoncu.

The secular television channel *Star* was among the first outlets to be turned into an AKP mouthpiece soon after the party's election. After defaulting to the TMSF, it was acquired in 2006 by a Turkish-Cypriot businessman who promptly "filled [it] with pro-AKP writers and editors,"[13] before transferring the company to Turkish mogul Ethem Sancak. In November 2013, Sancak acquired eleven additional media outlets, which were earlier seized by the TMSF.[14] A notorious pro-Erdoğan figure, Sancak not only declared that he has a "divine love" for Erdoğan on public television[15] and now serves on the AKP's executive committee, but has also publicly admitted to entering the media business primarily to support Erdoğan.[16]

Four years later, in 2017, Sancak sold his conglomerate to another member of the AKP, Zeki Yeşildağ,[17] who also serves on the Istanbul Municipality's city council. Yeşildağ and his brother Hasan are known to the Turkish public as Erdoğan's "voluntary bodyguards":[18] while Zeki reportedly took part in fights between members of Erdoğan's security team and protesters during the Turkish president's U.S. visits,[19] his brother Hasan deliberately committed a petty crime in 1998 just to be imprisoned together with Erdoğan and to act as Erdoğan personal guard behind bars.[20]

In 2008, meanwhile, Çalık Holding, where Erdoğan's son-in-law Berat Albayrak and his brother Serhat Albayrak were both senior executives, bought Turkey's second largest media group, Sabah-ATV, in a controversial $1.1 billion deal that was believed to be funded in part from abroad, specifically Germany and Qatar.[21] In August 2013, the brothers sold their media group – which by then controlled not only *Sabah* and *Takvim* but also the daily *Yeni Asır* and television broadcaster *A Haber* – to another pro-AKP business, the Kalyon Group.[22]

Corruption was a central driver in these acquisitions. Tapes leaked in December 2013 revealed that pro-AKP businesspeople had been pressured to pool money to fund the purchases.[23] In the tapes, Erdoğan appeared to manage the sale of Çalık Holding's media outlets to friendly businesspeople to whom he promised to offer tenders for public projects as a reward. They also revealed now-Prime Minister Binali Yıldırım's provision of funds to various businesspeople to facilitate the purchase of the media companies.[24] Directed by Erdoğan, an investigation report alleged, the AKP-led government promised construction tenders for high-speed rail, highway, tunnel, and airport projects to eight businesspeople, in return for a total of $630 million for this purpose.[25]

During the same period, Gülen-affiliated media bosses struck similar deals to expand their own media empire by acquiring secular and independent media outlets seized by the government's TMSF. Indeed, despite the movement's later public feud with Erdoğan, such acquisitions during the 2000s were very much part of the Islamist takeover of the Turkish media space. But in late 2013, upon the eruption of a massive corruption scandal that threatened to overthrow the AKP, Erdoğan pointed the finger of blame at Gülen and labeled his movement a terrorist organization. Gülen-affiliated media outlets responded by briefly turning anti-AKP and publishing reports selectively exposing the corruption of AKP officials. Erdoğan, in turn, cracked down on these groups, shuttering some of the outlets while bringing others formally under his fold. The results were pronounced; by September 2015, 18 companies owned by top Gülenists had come under TMSF's control.[26]

The government's takeover of pro-Gülen media also had implications for Turkey's image abroad. Having served as the AKP's top propaganda machine in the West for years, the Gülen movement's daily *Today's Zaman* – among the few English-language dailies to be run by Turkish journalists – has now been shut down. Today, the pro-Erdoğan newspaper *Daily Sabah*, which was founded by a pro-Erdoğan media group in February 2014 as a counterweight to *Today's Zaman*, serves among the most popular Turkish news sources in the English language.[27] Alongside the conspiratorial language common to Turkey's pro-government outlets, *Daily Sabah* portends to "appeal to 'the West' about what it gets wrong about Turkey."[28]

Coopting Turkey's official media

The Turkish Radio and Television Corporation (TRT), founded in 1964, is Turkey's national public broadcaster. By law, the corporation's funding comes from a contribution of two percent of all monthly electricity utility bills in Turkey. Last year, the broadcaster's reported budget was nearly $560 million (2 billion in Turkish Lira [TRY]), of which 86 percent came from these electricity consumption bills and revenues from taxes on electronic devices.[29]

Under Erdoğan's rule, however, TRT's external outreach grew massively between 2009 and 2015. The broadcaster established TRT Avaz in March 2009, which began broadcasting in Turkish, Azeri, Kazakh, Kyrgyz, Uzbek, and Turkmen, focusing on audiences in Central Asia, the Caucasus, the Balkans, and the Middle East. That October, TRT launched a documentary channel to promote Turkey, broadcasting in English, German, French, Russian, and Turkish, and in April 2010, it launched an Arabic-language channel as well.[30] In 2015, TRT launched its official English-language global news service, *TRT World.*[31]

The funding behind TRT's proliferating global outreach has been a controversial matter in Turkish politics. In 2016, TRT spent over $250 million (TRY 750 million) on external productions. Opposition lawmakers have claimed not only that these funds were transferred to pro-AKP companies and moguls,[32] but also that many of these purchases were kept secret for years before being aired – a case in point being the €4.5 million purchase of a TV series that was delivered to TRT in 2014 but never aired.[33] TRT's spending on external productions increased 49 percent the next year, totaling around $255 million (TRY 907 million) – more than half of that year's budget. The Turkish government admitted that TRT was purchasing nearly as many programs as it produced.[34]

Meanwhile Turkey's official news agency, Anadolu Agency, established in 1920,[35] has grown to launch 39 international offices around the world, with a network of correspondents in 86 countries.[36] While the agency was structured as a joint-stock company to ensure its autonomy,[37] it has come increasingly under Erdoğan's control in recent years. In 2011, Erdoğan appointed his former press advisor Kemal Öztürk as the agency's director general, subsequently replacing him with another former senior advisor, Şenol Kazancı, in 2014.[38] That year, two top editors for the agency's English-language department resigned from their posts, calling the agency "Erdoğan's propaganda mouthpiece."[39]

THE WEAPONIZATION OF TURKISH MEDIA

Once its colonization was complete, and Erdoğan's family and business cronies had successfully dominated Turkey's media sphere, the AKP-led government used its newfound powers to target and destroy its opponents at home and abroad. As the government's list of enemies evolved, the targets of pro-AKP gazettes and broadcasters evolved accordingly. A study of the last decade of AKP rule reveals a broad coalition of AKP opponents, both political and civil, that have tasted Erdoğan's medicine: Turkey's secular state bureaucracy, liberals, Kurds, religious minorities, and most recently the Gülen movement. Meanwhile, as Erdoğan's relationship with Europe and the United States frayed over the past half-decade, the targets of pro-government Turkish media expanded to include American and European politicians, states-people, journalists, and aid workers.

The pro-AKP media's attacks against these groups and individuals in the West, like the ones leveled against the groups and individuals at home, gained new strength after the failed coup attempt in Turkey in July 2016, and the ensuing state of emergency through which President Erdoğan has ruled ever since. But the trajectory of the AKP-controlled press over the last decade reveals more continuity than change in such practices, exposing the steady and increasing weaponization of Turkish media by the country's ruling elites against enemies both foreign and domestic.

The secular establishment

Perhaps the best example of how Erdoğan, together with his former allies in the Gülen movement, weaponized the media is his scheme to eliminate Turkey's secular establishment through two high profile show trials, Ergenekon and Balyoz, which mainly targeted the Turkish military and its secular nationalist allies.[40] Both cases were handled to a great extent by Gülen's followers in the police and judiciary, and involved the use of fabricated and planted evidence to frame numerous innocent individuals alongside a few authentic suspects.[41] Erdoğan put his political weight behind these cases, even going so far as to refer to himself as the "prosecutor" of the Ergenekon case in 2008.[42] In 2013, in two separate rulings of the Turkish Supreme Court of Appeals, 237 serving and retired members of the Turkish military were convicted of coup plotting as part of the Balyoz trial, while 251 defendants were convicted of membership in a secularist ultra-nationalist terrorist organization in the Ergenekon trial.[43]

In both cases, there was a systematic media campaign, especially in the pro-Gülen media, to frame and defame the suspects, as well as those who questioned the merits of the cases.[44] A detailed examination of the media coverage of the Balyoz case carried out by Harvard University's Dani Rodrik demonstrated that the Gülen movement's flagship daily, *Zaman*, and its English-language version, *Today's Zaman*, regularly published disinformation about the case.[45] When Rodrik started writing a blog and op-eds in international publications on these cases, he, too, was targeted in the same outlets and defamed as "a member of a global conspiracy," and as "a self-hating Jew in love with his executioner."[46]

The pro-Kurdish media

The mass trials for the Kurdistan Communities Union (KCK), a PKK-linked umbrella organization advocating "democratic confederalism" in Turkey, Iran, Iraq, and Syria, were another highly-politicized case carried out under AKP rule.[47] The investigations were launched in April of 2009, and culminated in the mass detention of Turkey's leading pro-Kurdish politicians, including 10 mayors, in December of that year.[48] Following their detention, the police lined the pro-Kurdish politicians up in front of the Diyarbakır courthouse in plastic handcuffs and arranged for journalists to take their photographs,[49] which could then be used by the pro-government media to humiliate them.[50] The defamation of pro-Kurdish politicians by the press became a key Kurdish grievance, highlighted the following year by the pro-Kurdish Peace and Democracy Party (BDP) in its campaign.[51] Publicly, however, the Turkish officials implicated in leaking the humiliating photographs denied the allegations.[52]

Significantly, the KCK trials also helped Erdoğan silence the pro-Kurdish media. In December of 2011, the Turkish government cracked down on pro-Kurdish outlets, including the Dicle News Agency (DİHA), as well as the dailies *Özgür Gündem* and *Azadiya Welat*, and arrested over 40 journalists. In September of 2012, these journalists were taken to court and charged with membership in the press council of the KCK.[53] Ultimately, the KCK trials were used by the pro-government media as a weapon to defame pro-Kurdish politicians, as well as to silence and shutter pro-Kurdish media.

Erdoğan's political opponents
The pro-AKP press has targeted the party's political opponents both individually and collectively as part of one large enemies network. Individually, opposition politicians have been smeared in pro-AKP gazettes, generally with charges that they are either immoral or corrupt. Collectively, they have been demonized as putschists, separatists, or terrorists through association with designated entities, such as the PKK, or the Fethullahist Terrorist Organization (FETÖ), the new designation given to the Gülen movement by the state following its falling out with Erdoğan.

The latest target of Erdoğan's political opponents has undoubtedly been Turkey's predominantly Kurdish Peoples' Democratic Party (HDP). Since its official inception in October of 2012, the HDP has presented a significant challenge to Erdoğan and the AKP by promoting ethnic, religious, gender, and cultural diversity in Turkey – an idea antithetical to the AKP. While the party's former iterations, which had a more Kurdish nationalist bent and composition, could secure no more than seven percent of the votes in elections, the HDP's co-chair Selahattin Demirtaş challenged Erdoğan in the 2014 presidential election, and remarkably won around 10 percent – indicating an electoral capacity for the HDP that surpassed the country's nation-wide election threshold of 10 percent for entering the parliament in a general election. Since the run-up to the June 2015 general elections, therefore, Turkey's Erdoğanist media focused its efforts on systematically smearing most HDP members as "terrorists" or "separatists," or both, and targeting many others as morally corrupt, un-Islamic, and un-Turkish.

Pro-AKP media also habitually lumps the HDP together with other political parties in order to tar all opposition with one brush. In fact, a key Islamist smear tactic is to highlight opposition parties' connection to the HDP – even that of the ultranationalist Nationalist Action Party (MHP), whose core ideology runs counter to the HDP's message of ethnic pluralism in Turkey. A clear example of this phenomenon appeared on the front page of the pro-government Turkish daily *Akşam* on June 5, 2015, two days before the general election that would cost the AKP its parliamentary majority for the first time in twelve years. The main headline, "The Dream Cabinet of the Mastermind," refers to a grand conspiracy theory promoted by Erdoğan and the AKP which, among other things, claimed that Jews have dominated the world for the past 3,500 years.[54] The "Mastermind" theory posits that global Jewry, together with a coalition of nefarious collaborators in Turkey and abroad, including Fethullah Gülen, freemasons, knights templar, the United States, United Kingdom, and Israel, conspire against the Turkish state and nation. The *Akşam* editors conveniently chose to highlight the conspiracy's purported representatives in Turkey – consisting of the AKP's three opposition parties in the Turkish parliament (the CHP, the HDP, and the MHP) as well as the outlawed PKK and the Marxist-Leninist Revolutionary People's Liberation Party/Front (DHKP/C).

After the HDP secured 13 percent of the votes in the June 2015 election, the Turkish government took more direct measures. It declared war anew on the PKK after a two-year respite in the fighting under the framework of the "Kurdish peace process." Erdoğan also declared a new round of snap elections for that November, in which he managed to secure anew a parliamentary majority for the AKP. Then, in the wake of the July 2016 coup attempt, the president used his emergency powers to imprison over a dozen HDP lawmakers, as well as hundreds of pro-HDP mayors from majority Kurdish towns.

Turkey's religious minorities

Since the failed coup attempt in 2016, Turkey's pro-AKP press has also targeted the country's religious minorities by associating them with the PKK or Gülen or the CIA or Israel, and either explicitly or implicitly sanctioning attacks against Turkey's non-Muslim citizens as the co-conspirators of an international scheme against the Turkish nation. This, despite the fact that the day after the abortive coup, the religious leaders of Turkey's Jewish, Armenian, Greek-Orthodox, and Syriac communities all denounced the attempt in a joint declaration,[55] and were joined later by representatives of Turkey's Muslim minority Alevi[56] and Shi'ite[57] faiths.

Such gestures, however, did little to mollify the country's pro-AKP media, which used the opportunity to connect the coup plot to Turkey's religious minorities. Two days after the abortive coup, a pro-government journalist writing for the pro-AKP *Yeni Asır* insisted that the coup's purported "mastermind," Fethullah Gülen, had a Jewish mother and an Armenian father, and was a member of the Catholic clerical hierarchy.[58]

Takvim, another pro-government daily, published a fabricated Vatican passport to "demonstrate" that Gülen was in fact a Catholic cardinal.[59] The daily *Akşam*, for its part, slandered the Greek-Orthodox ecumenical patriarch for "plotting" the abortive coup with the CIA, while a columnist at *Star* claimed that the plotters had been hiding in churches.[60]

Such incitement has led to attacks against religious minorities throughout the country. The first post-coup attacks took place against churches in Malatya and Trabzon – scenes of lethal attacks against Christians a decade ago.[61] Days after the failed coup attempt, mobs attacked the gates of the Saint Maria Catholic Church in Trabzon, a city on Turkey's Black Sea coast, with hammers, breaking the church's windows.[62] An Alevi worship hall there and homes in Malatya were next.[63] An Armenian high school in Istanbul was vandalized the following month, as reports emerged from the eastern Turkish province of Gaziantep about local harassment against Christian tourists.[64]

This past February, the Santa Maria Church was once again targeted – this time with an incendiary device that damaged the church's front door a day ahead of the anniversary of the 2006 assassination of the church's then-priest, Andrea Santoro.[65] Bishop Paolo Bizzeti, who assumed office as the vicar apostolic of Anatolia in 2015 – a seat vacant since the murder of his predecessor in 2010 – referred to the arson attempt as "one of the many episodes of intimidation and vandalism that affect the Trabzon church every week," complaining about assailants who regularly damage the gates and desecrate church grounds with trash.[66] Then, in March, a lone gunman fired a shot through Saint Maria's window, thus perpetrating the fifth confirmed attack against the church since Father Santoro's assassination.[67]

Individuals have also been targeted, smeared and slandered by the pro-AKP media. The fate of U.S. Pastor Andrew Brunson is a case in point; a Presbyterian minister from North Carolina who lived in Turkey as the head of an Izmir church for two decades, Brunson (together with his wife) was detained shortly after the coup attempt and placed in a maximum-security prison in Izmir.[68] He has been held there for almost two years, and could, under Turkey's draconian state of emergency, be held for up to five more (seven in total) in pre-trial detention.[69] He is accused of espionage and terrorism, as well as of plotting the 2016 coup.

Since his arrest, Turkey's pro-government media has been shameless in its smear campaign against Pastor Brunson. In May 2017, an author for the daily *Takvim* claimed that the pastor would have become the next director of the CIA had he been successful in helping to coordinate the attempted coup against Erdoğan.[70] Subsequently, in September, in a story titled "The Pastor's Bomb," *Takvim* similarly accused the CIA of masterminding the bomb attack against a shuttle bus carrying guards for the prison where Brunson was held, calling Brunson a CIA agent once again and dubbing the attack a "a message from the CIA" to the Turkish government.[71] Then, in December, the pro-AKP daily *Yeni Asır* published a story it called "FETÖ's Pastor Turns Out to Be a Fake," which asserted that Brunson was not a real pastor; that his documents were fake; that he operated as a spy; that he funded PKK sympathizers in the United States; that he received monthly payment from a U.S.-based foundation linked to FETÖ; and that he praised FETÖ in his sermons in İzmir.[72]

Turkey's state-run media has also been culpable in rising hate speech against religious minorities, using state funds for incitement against Jews and Christians, among others. *The Last Emperor* (*Payitaht Abdülhamid*), a historical drama funded and broadcasted by TRT, for example, is a blatantly anti-Semitic and anti-Christian drama.[73] The show melds Jewish conspiracies together with those surrounding the British Queen and other European powers, the Catholic Church, socialists, Young Turks and Freemasons into one overarching scheme against the Ottoman Empire – and the Turks.

Each episode, in turn, has led to an upsurge in hate speech and incitement online. One Twitter user, after watching this state-funded drama, vowed to turn the territory between the Euphrates and Nile rivers into Jewish graveyards.[74] Another Twitter user, after watching the drama said, "The more I watch *The Last Emperor*, the more my enmity to Jews increases. You infidels, you filthy creatures."[75]

Enemies abroad

Erdoğan comes from an Islamist tradition that sees the West, portrayed as the morally-corrupt Judeo-Christian world, as the archenemy.[76] Although Erdoğan came to power in 2002 by toning down his anti-Western rhetoric, and even embracing – albeit tactically – Turkey's European Union membership, he returned to his virulent anti-Western rhetoric once he consolidated power and no longer felt the need to dissimulate to gain votes and legitimacy. Hence, Americans and Europeans have ascended to the top of Erdoğan's foreign enemies list in recent years.

The primary complaint of AKP officials and their publicists in the media has centered on the U.S. military alliance with Kurdish rebels in Syria in the fight against the Islamic State. Meanwhile, Fethullah Gülen's residence in the United States has led to further Turkish grievances against America; since the failed coup attempt in July 2016, the AKP media has accused Washington of plotting the putsch together with Gülen.[77] Since that summer, Turkey's pro-government newspapers have likewise been littered with anti-American rhetoric built around conspiracy theories in which the CIA and the U.S. Army, often in cooperation with European states, work to undermine Turkey's national security. These conspiracies, in turn, have helped spread anti-Americanism among the Turkish people.

Thus, with Erdoğan's apparent sanction, Turkey's state-owned media continuously levels accusations against the U.S. regarding its cooperation with Syrian Kurds, framing the partnership not as one formed to defeat the Islamic State but rather as part of a conspiracy against the Turkish state and nation. In February 2018, for example, the Anadolu Agency published a report arguing that the U.S. could be tried in international courts for "being a terrorist state" for its support to the PKK's Syrian wing.[78] The following month, it published an expose on the PKK's reinforcements sent to the Kurdish-ruled Syrian town of Afrin, where the Turkish army carried out an operation, framing the finding as a revelation of the U.S. "plot" to disguise the PKK's operations.[79]

This animus toward Washington's Syrian and Kurdish policies often blend with grievances over the alleged U.S. complicity in the July 2016 coup attempt. In a telling November 2017 piece in *Sabah*, columnist Ersin Ramoğlu argued that the U.S. planning of the coup attempt "could even lead to war with America... FETÖ was going to create public indignation, and hand the country, along with Erdoğan, over to the infidel. America gave this order to Gülen."[80] He likewise added that "it is certain" the United States had "founded the Islamic State" – as an excuse to partner with the Kurds/PKK against Turkey.[81] Such sentiments are echoed in other articles published in Turkey's pro-government media outlets, which demonize the United States as a whole, as well as individual Americans, based on an array of complaints.

ENDURING APPEAL

When Erdoğan's AKP rose to power in Turkey in 2002, few observers imagined it would rule the country for over 15 years. Not only was Turkey a democratic country with periodic elections, but the successive coalition governments of the 1990s testified to a deeply divided electorate, no part of which could claim more than a quarter of the public's support. Moreover, throughout the history of the modern Turkish republic, even the most authoritarian-minded politicians had never succeeded in keeping their positions of power for more than a decade; all were eventually ousted, either by the ballot box or by a military coup. Indeed, even the most successful politicians lost their popular appeal at some point in their careers.

Analysts therefore have scrambled to explain Erdoğan's enduring electoral popularity. Some have pointed to the AKP's political successes: rehabilitating the crumbling economy of the 1990s, extending public services and social transfers to Turkey's previously neglected communities, dampening the Turkish state's age-old militant secularism in favor of extending religious freedom to the country's Sunni Muslim majority, and entering into dialogue with the PKK for peace. The most potent evidence for this view is the AKP's wide electoral reach; today, the party appeals to nearly half of the Turkish electorate, only a small fraction of which holds Islamist ideals.

Others have focused on the more disreputable aspects of Erdoğan's power politics to explain his ostensibly unwavering public appeal: clientelism and micro-management. Indeed, juxtaposed with his modest socio-economic upbringing, the Turkish strongman's current riches are bewildering. His children hide their wealth in off-shore accounts, while his "shopaholic" wife is notorious for shutting down stores during her visits to European capitals to spend hundreds of thousands of dollars on clothes, make-up, and accessories.[82]

This newfound wealth, in turn, affords Erdoğan a powerful weapon that he skillfully has used against both political opponents and international critics: ownership and management of the country's public and private press. Having spent a decade colonizing 90 percent of the Turkish media, he uses it to boost his propaganda, to justify his autocratic actions, to conceal or dilute his scandalous corruption, and to defame, criminalize, and eliminate his enemies.

More fundamentally, Erdoğan's media empire allows him to dismantle Turkey's democratic order and institute his own in its place. Having secured near-total control at home, the strongman is now likely to re-focus his attention on challenging the Western-led liberal order – which he sees as a threat to his own regime – on the international stage. Thus Turkey, though nominally a NATO ally, must be understood to have weaponized its media in much the same way as have Erdogan's fellow autocrats in Iran and Russia: as a tool of both domestic intimidation and international influence.

ENDNOTES

1. These conglomerates are Ahmet Albayrak's Albayrak, Turgay Ciner's Ciner, Erdoğan Demirören's Demirören, Ferit Şahenk's Doğuş, Mücahit Ören's İhlas, Zeki Yeşildağ's Tmedya, and Cemal Kalyoncu's Turkuvaz.

2. "Doğan Medya grubu Demirören'e satıldı (Doğan Media Group sold to Demirören)," *BirGün* (Istanbul), March 21, 2018, https://www.birgun.net/haber-detay/dogan-medya-grubu-demiroren-e-satildi-208892.html.

3. Elif Akgül, "Olağanüstü Hal'in Basın Bilançosu (The media tally of the 'state of emergency')," *Bianet* (Istanbul), December 7, 2016, https://m.bianet.org/bianet/ifade-ozgurlugu/181480-olaganustu-hal-in-basin-bilancosu.

4. "AKP iktidarının 15 yılında 535 gazeteci tutuklandı (535 journalists detained under 15 years of AKP rule)," *Cumhuriyet* (Istanbul), May 3, 2018, http://www.cumhuriyet.com.tr/haber/siyaset/968345/AKP_iktidarinin_15_yilinda_535_gazeteci_tutuklandi.html.

5. Zia Weise, "Turkey jails more journalists than any other nation. Those in detention are all terrorists, Erdoğan says," *PRI*, June 28, 2017, https://www.pri.org/stories/2017-06-28/turkey-jails-more-journalists-any-other-nation-those-detention-are-all-terrorists.

6. Andrew Finkel, "Captured News Media: The Case of Turkey," Center for International Media Assistance, National Endowment for Democracy, October 2015, http://www.cima.ned.org/wp-content/uploads/2015/10/CIMA-Captured-News-Media_The-Case-of-Turkey.pdf.

7. Mehmet Ali Birand, "Nihayet, bir komutan 'Andıç hata idi' dedi... (Finally a commander said 'Andıç was a mistake')," *Hürriyet* (Istanbul), May 9, 2009, http://www.hurriyet.com.tr/nihayet-bir-komutan-andic-hata-idi-dedi-11612952.

8. Nedim Şener, "Kanal 7'deki karmaşık ilişkiler (Complicated relationships at Channel 7)," *Milliyet* (Istanbul), August 21, 2010, http://www.milliyet.com.tr/kanal---nin-gizli-yuzu-/guncel/haberdetayarsiv/21.08.2010/988581/default.htm.

9. "Kanal 7'nin öyküsü (Channel 7's story)," *T24* (Istanbul), September 30, 2008, http://t24.com.tr/haber/kanal-7nin-oykusu,9491.

10. "Kanal 7 nasıl kuruldu? (How was Channel 7 established?)," *Vatan* (Istanbul), September 28, 2008, http://www.gazetevatan.com/kanal-7-nasil-kuruldu--201116-ekstra/.

11. "Zaman," *Media Ownership Monitor Turkey*, n.d. (accessed February 13, 2018), https://turkey.mom-rsf.org/en/media/detail/outlet/zaman/; "About Us," *Zaman* (Istabul), April 29, 2016, https://web.archive.org/web/20160429085929/http://arsiv.zaman.com.tr/argit3/ss/aboutus.htm.

12. Ibid.

13. Tuba Eldem, "The transformation of the media sector from above: Implications for the freedom of media in Turkey," in Sai Felicia Krishna-Hensel, ed., *Authoritarian and Populist Influences in the New Media* (Routledge, 2017), https://books.google.com/books?id=ZYU0DwAAQBAJ&.

14. "State-seized media assets of Çukurova conglomerate sold to businessman Ethem Sancak," *Hürriyet Daily News*, November 22, 2013, http://www.hurriyetdailynews.com/state-seized-media-assets-of-cukurova-conglomerate-sold-to-businessman-ethem-sancak-58344

15. "Ethem Sancak: Erdoğan'ı gördükçe aşık oldum, böyle bir ilahi aşk iki erkek arasında olabiliyor (Ethem Sancak: I fell in love with Erdoğan when I saw him, such a divine love between two men is possible)," *T24* (Istanbul), May 15, 2015, http://t24.com.tr/haber/ethem-sancak-Erdoğani-gordukce-asik-oldum-boyle-bir-ilahi-ask-iki-erkek-arasinda-olabiliyor,296777.

16. "Ethem Sancak Group," *Media Ownership Monitor Turkey*, n.d. (accessed February 6, 2018), https://turkey.mom-rsf.org/en/owners/companies/detail/company/company/show/ethem-sancak-group/.

17. "ABD'deki koruma kavgasının organizatörü Zeki Yeşildağ medya patronu oldu (Organizer of the bodyguard brawl in the U.S. Zeki Yesildag became media boss)," *Cumhuriyet* (Istanbul), September 6, 2017, http://www.cumhuriyet.com.tr/haber/turkiye/818033/ABD_deki_koruma_kavgasinin_organizatoru_Zeki_Yesildag_medya_patronu_oldu.html.

18. Erdoğan'ın gönüllü fedaisi medya patronu oldu (Erdoğan's voluntary bodyguard became a media boss)," *Cumhuriyet* (Istanbul), August 17, 2017, http://www.cumhuriyet.com.tr/haber/turkiye/805269/Erdoğan_in_gonullu_fedaisi_medya_patronu_oldu.html.

19. "Erdoğan'ı koruyan ekibi yöneten o isim kim (Who is the person that manages Erdoğan's security team)," *Oda TV* (Istanbul), April 1, 2016, https://odatv.com/Erdoğani-koruyan-ekibi-yo-

neten-o-isim-kim-0104161200.html;

20. "Erdoğan'ın gönüllü fedaisi medya patronu oldu (Erdoğan's voluntary bodyguard became a media boss)," *Cumhuriyet* (Istanbul), August 17, 2017, http://www.cumhuriyet.com.tr/haber/turkiye/805269/Erdoğan_in_gonullu_fedaisi_medya_patronu_oldu.html.

21. "Company Overview of Sabah-ATV Media Group," Bloomberg, February 7, 2018, https://www.bloomberg.com/research/stocks/private/snapshot.asp?privcapId=43976352; Sibel Yerdeniz, "Deniz Feneri'nden 'ampul'e yüzyılın aydınlanma hareketi (1) (The greatest enlightenment of the century from Deniz Feneri to 'the lightbulb' – Part 1)," *T24* (Istanbul), January 16, 2014, http://t24.com.tr/yazarlar/bilinmeyen/deniz-fenerinden-ampule-yuzyilin-aydinlanma-hareketi,8308; "Turkish media group Sabah-ATV sold to Kalyon group," *Hürriyet Daily News*, December 20, 2013, http://www.hurriyetdailynews.com/turkish-media-group-sabah-atv-sold-to-kalyon-group-59898; Craig Shaw and Zeynep Sentek, "Turkish President Erdoğan's son-in-law in off-shore tax scheme," *The Black Sea* (Bucharest), May 19, 2017, https://theblacksea.eu/malta-files/article/en/Erdoğans-son-in-law-off-shore-tax-scheme; Zülfikar Doğan, "Amid financial hardship, Erdoğan looks to Qatar as 'rich daddy,'" *Al-Monitor*, December 29, 2015, http://www.al-monitor.com/pulse/en/originals/2015/12/turkey-israel-russia-qatari-money-props-up-Erdoğan.html.

22. "Sabah ve ATV Kalyon'a satıldı (Sabah and ATV sold to Kalyon)," *Hürriyet* (Istanbul), December 12, 2013, http://www.hurriyet.com.tr/sabah-ve-atv-kalyona-satildi-25407253.

23. Eldem, "The transformation of the media sector from above."

24. "Kalyon Group," *Media Ownership Monitor Turkey*, n.d. (accessed February 2, 2018), https://turkey.mom-rsf.org/en/owners/companies/detail/company/company/show/kalyon-group/.

25. "Erdoğan istedi, yüz milyonlar toplandı (Erdoğan asked for it, hundreds of millions were collected)," *Diken* (Istanbul), February 1, 2014, http://www.diken.com.tr/Erdoğan-istedi-sabah-atv-icin-milyarlar-toplandi/.

26. "State fund 'takes control of Koza-İpek Holding's 18 companies in failed coup attempt probe," *Hürriyet Daily News*, September 9, 2016, http://www.hurriyetdailynews.com/state-fund-takes-control-of-koza-ipek-holdings-18-companies-in-failed-coup-attempt-probe-103748.

27. Burcu Aldinç, "Türkiye'yi dünyaya DAILY SABAH anlatacak (Daily Sabah will tell the world about Turkey)," *Sabah* (Istanbul), March 2, 2014, https://www.sabah.com.tr/pazar/2014/03/02/turkiyeyi-dunyaya-daily-sabah-anlatacak; Emre Aköz, "New English daily offers Turkish government perspective," *Al-Monitor*, February 27, 2014, https://www.al-monitor.com/pulse/en/politics/2014/02/turkey-new-english-newspaper-government-perspective.html.

28. William Armstrong, "Army of Spin," *Foreign Policy*, December 9, 2014, https://foreignpolicy.com/2014/12/09/army-of-spin-turkey-media-Erdoğan/.

29. "Gelirinin yüzde 86'sını halk veriyor... TRT'den milyonlarca liralık zarar, (The public funds 86 percent of its revenues... TRT's loss of millions of lira)," *Cumhuriyet* (Istanbul), January 23, 2017, http://www.cumhuriyet.com.tr/haber/turkiye/664342/Gelirinin_yuzde_86_sini_halk_veriyor..._TRT_den_milyonlarca_liralik_zarar.html.

30. "Tarihçe (History)," *TRT* (Ankara), n.d., http://www.trt.net.tr/Kurumsal/Tarihce.aspx.

31. "Turkey: TRT World launches test broadcast," *Anadolu Agency* (Ankara), May 18, 2015, http://aa.com.tr/en/turkey/turkey-trt-world-launches-test-broadcast/45995.

32. "7 bin personeli olan TRT yandaşlara servet dağıtmış (TRT with 7 thousand staff members distributed a fortune to partisans)," *Cumhuriyet* (Istanbul), August 3, 2017, http://www.cumhuriyet.com.tr/haber/siyaset/795372/7_bin_personeli_olan_TRT_yandaslara_servet_dagitmis.html.

33. "TRT, son 10 yılda 3.455 kurum dışı yapım satın aldı (TRT purchased 3455 external productions in the last 10 years)," *T24* (Istanbul), January 22, 2018, http://t24.com.tr/haber/trt-son-10-yilda-3455-kurum-disi-yapim-satin-aldi,542187.

34. "Gelirinin yüzde 86'sını halk veriyor... TRT'den milyonlarca liralık zarar, (The public funds 86 percent of its revenues... TRT's loss of millions of lira)."

35. "History," *Anadolu Agency* (Ankara), n.d., http://aa.com.tr/en/p/history.

36. "International Offices," *Anadolu Agency* (Ankara), n.d., http://aa.com.tr/en/p/international-offices;"Anadolu Agency's language and news network strengthens," *Anadolu Agency* (Ankara), October 27, 2017, http://aa.com.tr/en/corporate-news/anadolu-agency-s-language-and-news-network-strengthens/949207v.

37. "Your Source for Trusted News," *Anadolu Agency* (Ankara), n.d., https://www.aa.com.tr/uploads/TempUserFiles/Kurumsal/Katalog_en.pdf.

38. "Senol Kazanci appointed AA's new Director General," *Anadolu Agency* (Turkey), December 16, 2014, http://aa.com.tr/en/turkey/senol-kazanci-appointed-aas-new-director-general/92145.

39. Kate O'Sullivan and Laura Benitez, "We Quit Working for Erdoğan's Propaganda Mouthpiece," *Vice*, April 8, 2014, https://www.vice.com/en_uk/article/kwp7aa/inside-Erdoğans-propaganda-mouthpiece.

40. Gareth Jenkins, "The Balyoz Retrial and the Changing Politics of Turkish Justice," *The Turkey Analyst*, June 25, 2014, https://www.turkeyanalyst.org/publications/turkey-analyst-articles/item/331-the-balyoz-retrial-and-the-changing-politics-of-turkish-justice.html.

41. Gareth Jenkins, "The Ergenekon Verdicts: Chronicle of an Injustice Foretold," *The Turkey Analyst*, August 14, 2013, https://www.turkeyanalyst.org/publications/turkey-analyst-articles/item/50-the-ergenekon-verdicts-chronicle-of-an-injustice-foretold.html.

42. "Evet Ergenkon'un savcısıyım (Yes I am the prosecutor of Ergenekon)," *Vatan* (Istanbul), July 16, 2008, http://www.gazetevatan.com/-evet-ergenekon-un-savcisiyim--189246-siyaset.

43. Jenkins, "The Balyoz Retrial and the Changing Politics of Turkish Justice."

44. Gareth Jenkins, "From Fear to Absurdity: Turkey's Continuing Politicized Court Cases," *The Turkey Analyst*, April 10, 2013, https://www.turkeyanalyst.org/publications/turkey-analyst-articles/item/39-from-fear-to-absurdity-turkeys-continuing-politicized-court-cases.html.

45. Dani Rodrik, "The Plot Against the Generals," personal blog, June 2014, http://drodrik.scholar.harvard.edu/files/dani-rodrik/files/plot-against-the-generals.pdf.

46. Ibid.

47. Gareth Jenkins, "The Latest KCK Arrests: One Step Closer to Breaking Point," *The Turkey Analyst*, November 7, 2011, https://www.turkeyanalyst.org/publications/turkey-analyst-articles/item/282-the-latest-kck-arrests-one-step-closer-to-breaking-point.html.

48. "Kelepçeli açılım hatırası... (Memory of an opening with handcuffs)," *Radikal* (Istanbul), December 26, 2009, http://www.radi-

kal.com.tr/politika/kelepceli-acilim-hatirasi-971177.

49. Tolga Korkut, "'Bu Fotoğraf Kürt Siyasetçileri Aşağılamak İçin Yaratıldı (This photograph was created to belittle Kurdish politicians),'" *Bianet* (Istanbul), December 28, 2009, http://bianet.org/bianet/insan-haklari/119129-bu-fotograf-kurt-siyasetcileri-asagilamak-icin-yaratildi.

50. Muharrem Erbey, "Kürtlerin kelepçeyle imtihanında kaybeden hep devlet oldu (In the testing of the Kurds through handcuffs, the loser has always been the state)," *Ahval* (Gibraltar), December 26, 2017, https://ahvalnews.com/tr/kck-operasyonlari/kurtlerin-kelepceyle-imtihaninda-kaybeden-hep-devlet-oldu.

51. Cem Emir and Bayram Bulut, "Kelepçe fotoğrafları billboardlarda (Their photos with handcuffs are on the billboards)," *Hürriyet* (Istanbul), January 1, 2010, http://www.hurriyet.com.tr/gundem/kelepce-fotograflari-bilbordlarda-13360157.

52. "Atalay 'kelepçeli fotoğraf' iddiasını yalanladı (Atalay falsifies the "handcuffed photo" allegations)," *Sabah* (Istanbul), March 27, 2014, https://www.sabah.com.tr/gundem/2014/03/27/atalay-kelepceli-fotograf-iddiasini-yalanladi.

53. "'KCK Basın Komitesi' Davası Başlıyor (The KCK press committee trial begins)," *Bianet* (Istanbul), August 16, 2012, https://bianet.org/bianet/ifade-ozgurlugu/140352-kck-basin-komitesi-davasi-basliyor.

54. Ariel Ben Solomon, "Turkish 'Documentary' Says Jews Have Been 'Mastermind' For 3,500 Years," *Jerusalem Post*, April 16, 2015, https://www.jpost.com/Middle-East/Turkish-documentary-says-Jews-have-been-mastermind-for-3500-years-398299.

55. "Religious leaders stand together against coup attempt in Turkey," *Hürriyet Daily News*, July 16, 2016, http://www.hurriyetdailynews.com/religious-leaders-stand-together-against-coup-attempt-in-turkey-101690.

56. "Tek çıkış yolu demokrasi (Democracy is the only way out)," *Cumhuriyet* (Istanbul), July 16, 2016, http://www.cumhuriyet.com.tr/haber/turkiye/568631/Tek_cikis_yolu_demokrasi.html.

57. "Halkın İradesine Darbeye Hayır (No to the coup against the people's will)," *Caferi ve Ehl-i Beyt Derneği*, July 21, 2016, http://www.ehlibeytder.com/kursumuz/halkin-iradesine-darbeye-hayir-h3712.html.

58. Can Kemal Özer, "Şerefli Milletin Yiğit Evlatları Tarih Yazdı (The honorable nation's brave children make history)," *Yeni Söz* (Istan-

bul), July 17, 2016, http://www.yenisoz.com.tr/serefli-mille-tin-yigit-evlatlari-tarih-yazdi-makale-14422.

59. "Feto'ya kardinal pasaportu verildi (Cardinal passport given to Feto)," *Takvim* (Istanbul), October 8, 2016, https://www.takvim.com.tr/guncel/2016/10/08/fetoya-kardinal-pasaportu-verildi.

60. "Turkish press accuses Bartholomew of complicity in failed coup," *Vatican Insider*, September 1, 2016, http://www.lastampa.it/2016/09/01/vaticaninsider/eng/world-news/turk-ish-press-accuses-bartholomew-of-complicity-in-failed-coup-nS-sF1RHaikPpZTR7YQSQLO/pagina.html; Ersoy Dede, "Firari general, kayıp G3'ler! (Fugitive general, missing G3s!)" *Star* (Istanbul), August 3, 2016, http://www.star.com.tr/yazar/firari-gener-al-kayip-g3ler-yazi-1130644.

61. "Turkey: churches targeted during attempted coup," *World Watch Monitor*, July 19, 2016, https://www.worldwatchmonitor.org/2016/07/turkey-churches-targeted-during-attempted-coup.

62. "Church Attacks in Malatya and Trabzon," *Agos* (Istanbul), July 18, 2016, http://www.agos.com.tr/en/article/15936/church-at-tacks-in-trabzon-and-malatya.

63. "Tension rises in eastern Turkish province amid reports of march on Alevi neighborhoods," *Hürriyet Daily News*, July 18, 2016, http://www.hurriyetdailynews.com/tension-rises-in-eastern-turkish-prov-ince-amid-reports-of-march-on-alevi-neighborhoods-101758.

64. Miran Manukyan, "Tıbrevank'ın duvarına ırkçı yazı (Racist writing on Tibrevank's wall)," *Agos* (Istanbul), August 13, 2016, http://www.agos.com.tr/tr/yazi/16213/tibrevankin-duvarina-irkci-yazi; "Gaziantep'te Uzakdoğulu turistlere 'tepki': Müslümanları Hris-tiyan yapıyorsunuz, gavurlar! ('Reaction' to Far Eastern tourists in Gaziantep: You infidels turn Muslims into Christians)" *Diken* (Istanbul), August 18, 2016, http://www.diken.com.tr/gazian-tepte-uzakdogulu-turistlere-tepki-muslumanlari-hristiyan-yapiyor-sunuz-gavurlar.

65. "Turchia, ordigno incendiario contro la chiesa di don Andrea Santoro a Trabzon (Incendiary bomb against the church of Don Andrea Santoro in Trabzon, Turkey)," *Vatican Insider*, February 7, 2018, http://www.lastampa.it/2018/02/07/vaticaninsid-er/ita/nel-mondo/turchia-ordigno-incendiario-contro-la-chie-sa-di-don-andrea-santoro-a-trabzon-YIRbJzWJPDdOc0MEY-ZC50K/pagina.html.

66. "Turkey, the Pope: the Jesuit Bizzeti in the office that belonged

to Padovese," *Vatican Insider*, August 14, 2015, http://www. lastampa.it/2015/08/14/vaticaninsider/eng/world-news/turkey-the-pope-the-jesuit-bizzeti-in-the-office-that-belonged-to-padovese-ZqnciZ8f0z8JPMQjd0JL3N/pagina.html); Rachel Donadio, "Catholic Bishop Stabbed in Turkey," *New York Times*, June 3, 2010, https://www.nytimes.com/2010/06/04/world/europe/04bishop.html; "Fetö'nün papazı sahte çıktı (FETÖ's pastor turned out to be a fake)," *Yeni Asır* (Izmir), December 26, 2017, https://www.yeniasir.com.tr/surmanset/2017/12/27/fetonunpapazi-sahte-cikti; "Trabzon'daki Kiliseye Her Hafta Saldırı Oluyor (There is an attack against the church in Trabzon every week)," *Haber 61* (Trabzon), February 7, 2018, https://www.haber61.net/trabzon/trabzon-daki-kiliseye-her-hafta-saldiri-oluyor-h315192. html.

67. "Attack on Saint Maria Catholic Church in Trabzon," *Bianet* (Istanbul), March 7, 2018, http://m.bianet.org/english/minorities/194935-attack-on-saint-maria-catholic-church-in-trabzon.

68. Aykan Erdemir and Eric Edelman, *Erdogan's Hostage Diplomacy: Western Nationals in Turkish Prisons* (FDD Press, 2018), http://www.defenddemocracy.org/content/uploads/documents/REPORT_Erdogan_Hostages.pdf.

69. United States Commission on International Religious Freedom, "Press Release: Turkey Misses Opportunity to Release Pastor Andrew Brunson, Sets Next Hearing to May 7," April 16, 2018, http://www.uscirf.gov/news-room/press-releases-statements/turkey-misses-opportunity-release-pastor-andrew-brunson-sets.

70. Mevlüt Yüksel, "15 Temmuz başarılı olsaydı CIA'nın başına geçecekti (Had July 15 succeeded, he would have ascended to the head of CIA)," *Takvim* (Istanbul), May 20, 2017, https://www.takvim.com.tr/guncel/2017/05/20/15-temmuz-basarili-olsaydi-cianin-basina-gececekti.

71. "'Pastör' bombası (The pastor's bomb)," *Takvim* (Istanbul), September 1, 2017, https://www.takvim.com.tr/guncel/2017/09/01/pastor-bombasi.

72. "Fetö'nün papazı sahte çıktı (FETÖ's pastor turned out to be a fake)," *Yeni Asır* (Izmir), December 26, 2017, https://www.yeniasir.com.tr/surmanset/2017/12/27/fetonun-papazi-sahte-cikti.

73. Aykan Erdemir and Oren Kessler, "A Turkish TV blockbuster reveals Erdoğan's conspiratorial, anti-Semitic worldview," *Washington Post*, May 15, 2018, https://www.washingtonpost.com/news/

democracy-post/wp/2017/05/15/a-turkish-tv-blockbuster-reveals-Erdoğans-conspiratorial-anti-semitic-worldview.

74. Fettah Karayel, "#HainlerinSonu Senn yarım bıraktığn o işi evelAL-LAH torunlarn gerçekleştirecek ve Fırat/Nil arasını Yahudi mezarlığı yapacak ecdadım Osmanlı [sic] (#EndtoTraitors Your grandchildren will finish that job you left incomplete and will turn the Euphrates/Nile into a Jewish cemetery, my ancestors are Ottoman)," Twitter message dated April 10, 2017 (accessed on March 17, 2017), https://web.archive.org/web/20170510194952/https:/twitter.com/KarayelFettah/status/842825131760193537.

75. Serdar Korucu, "Antisemit Mesajlar Payitaht'ın 4. Bölümü Üzerinden Sürdü (The anti-Semitic messages continue in Payitaht's 4th episode)," *Avlaremoz* (Istanbul), March 23, 2017, http://www.avlaremoz.com/2017/03/23/antisemit-mesajlar-payitahtin-4-bolumu-uzerinden-surdu-serdar-korucu.

76. Soner Çağaptay, "Turkey's Ties to the West are in Deep Trouble," *The Cipher Brief*, April 14, 2017, https://www.thecipherbrief.com/column_article/turkeys-ties-to-the-west-are-in-deep-trouble-2.

77. "FETÖ'nün darbe girişiminde CIA'nın rolü deşifre oldu (CIA's role in FETÖ's coup attempt deciphered)," *Yeni Şafak*, July 18, 2016, https://www.yenisafak.com/dunya/fetonun-darbe-girisiminde-cia-nin-rolu-desifre-oldu-2495712.

78. "ABD terör devleti olmaktan yargılanabilir (The U.S. can be tried for being a terrorist state)," *Anadolu Agency* (Ankara), February 15, 2018, https://aa.com.tr/tr/dunya/abd-teror-devleti-olmaktan-yargilanabilir/1063821.

79. "Zeytin Dalı Harekatı ABD'nin SDG oyununu açığa çıkardı (Operation Olive Branch revealed the U.S.'s SDF plot)," *Anadolu Agency* (Ankara), March 5, 2018, https://aa.com.tr/tr/dunya/zeytin-dali-harekati-abdnin-sdg-oyununu-aciga-cikardi/1080648.

80. Ersin Ramoğlu, "Darbenin taşlarını böyle döşediler (Here's how they laid the groundwork for the coup)," *Sabah* (Istanbul), November 21, 2017, https://www.sabah.com.tr/bolgeler/yazarlar/ramoglu/2017/11/21/darbenin-taslarini-boyle-dosediler.

81. Ibid.

82. Dorian Jones, "Turkish Opposition Claims Erdoğan's Family Hid Money Offshore," *Voice of America*, November 28, 2017, https://www.voanews.com/a/turkey-opposition-claims-recep-tayyip-Erdoğan-family-hid-money-offshore/4140478.html; "Emine Erdoğan shopping spree stops traffic in Brussels," *The Bulletin* (Brussels), Oc-

tober 7, 2015, https://www.thebulletin.be/emine-Erdoğan-shopping-spree-stops-traffic-brussels; Paul Thompson, "The £43m-a-year President, his 'shopaholic' wife and their £2,000 per roll silk wallpaper in the bathroom: Inside Turkey tyrant's £500million palace... so dripping in gold 'it would have even made Saddam blush,'" *The Daily Mail*, July 18, 2016, http://www.dailymail.co.uk/news/article-3696037/She-silk-wallpaper-bathroom-2-000-roll-Super-spending-habits-Turkey-tyrant-s-shopaholic-wife-laid-bare-two-million-coup-hit-country-earn-3-day.html.

QATAR'S SOFT POWER EXPERIMENT
Jonathan Schanzer and Varsha Koduvayur

Al-Jazeera, the Doha-based satellite television network, first hit the airwaves in 1996. More than two decades later, the channel has become synonymous with the nation of Qatar itself. Originally beamed into the homes of millions of Arabs, later expansions have broadened the channel's reach into Europe and the United States. In the process, *Al-Jazeera* has almost single-handedly transformed the tiny Gulf state that sponsors it into a regional heavyweight, enabling the ruling regime in Doha to project its vision and influence on a vast regional and global scale.

In its early days, *Al-Jazeera* redefined television programming in a region dominated by bland government propaganda. The channel aired lively debates featuring opposition voices never seen on Arab screens before, like those of Israeli officials and Gulf dissidents. But *Al-Jazeera* has also played a malign role, from supporting al-Qaeda and the insurgency in Iraq to backing Hamas in Gaza or the Muslim Brotherhood during the Arab Spring. Indeed, the channel's initial edginess – embodied in its slogan, "the opinion and the other opinion" – has sadly given way to advocacy for Qatar's foreign policy objectives.

BIRTH OF A MOUTHPIECE

Hamad bin Khalifa al Thani became *emir* of Qatar in 1995 by overthrowing his father, Khalifa, in a bloodless coup. The event was jarring for the region's conservative hereditary monarchies, which all supported the deposed Khalifa, because "no one wanted to set a precedent of a son unseating a father."[1] In fact, Saudi Arabia allegedly backed at least one counter-coup, an event that epitomized the bad blood that still exists between Doha and Riyadh today.[2]

Less than a year after taking power, Hamad created *Al-Jazeera* in February of 1996, and the station began its first broadcast on November 1st of that year.[3] *Al-Jazeera*'s rise was born of Hamad's rejection of his father's belief that Qatar would benefit most if the emirate never "moved too far ahead of others in the region, culturally, economically or politically." Hamad saw things differently. His belief that Qatar should be "known and noticed" reflected his ambition for the country to become a presence on the world stage.[4] It is for this reason that he did not simply modernize the existing terrestrial *Qatari TV*, but instead launched a new satellite channel to compete with the likes of *CNN* and the BBC.[5]

Hamad's motives for establishing *Al-Jazeera* may also have been to create a tool of asymmetric power with which to challenge the Saudis, reflecting his disdain for the kingdom and the counter-coup he accused Saudi Arabia of sponsoring. From its infancy, *Al-Jazeera* gave a platform to Saudi dissidents and criticized the kingdom's "leadership as never before," which thoroughly irked Riyadh.[6]

Around the time of *Al-Jazeera*'s launch, Saudi Arabia and the BBC were working on a joint venture. But in April 1996, this project fell apart over Saudi anger at how the BBC reported on the kingdom. *Al-Jazeera* absorbed the staff and journalists from the failed venture, poaching a talented cadre of Western-trained journalists with extensive knowledge of "Arab politics and audiences"[7] – a move that almost certainly further infuriated the Saudis.

Al-Jazeera "struck like lightning" in the region. Until then, Arabs had largely ignored domestic Arab media, given the preponderance of government-controlled stations that parroted official views.[8] For objective reporting, Arabs turned to Western networks like the BBC or *CNN*, but they could not watch them in Arabic. *Al-Jazeera*, broadcast in Arabic and based in an Arab country, and with primarily Arab staff, became a source of pride to Arabs.[9]

Al-Jazeera also capitalized on the satellite television boom across the Middle East in the 1990s. Developments in satellite technology – including the popularity of a new band (Ku) for direct-to-home broadcasting, and the launch of new and more powerful satellites – increased the capacity to broadcast to the Arab world while also increasing affordability, thus opening the door to a new generation of viewers.[10]

The network was the first Arab channel to feature Israelis. Other regional stations either ignored Israelis or spoke for them. *Al-Jazeera* allowed them to speak for themselves. As Walid al-Omary, the former Ramallah bureau chief, observed, "many in the Arab world had never heard an Israeli voice."[11] Some cynically believed that the goal was simply to garner more viewers by giving voice to the Israelis, whom Arabs loved to hate. Others believed this was a potential path to peace or normalization. Whatever the motivation, the policy did not come without a price. Indeed, an extremist group called the Organization of Revolutionary Cells-Arab Gulf bombed a Qatar Airways office in Beirut in the summer of 2001 to protest *Al-Jazeera*'s policy of providing airtime to Israelis.[12]

But the network did not need Israel to generate controversy. It tackled taboo political, religious, economic, or social topics with zest and aplomb. In *The Opposite Direction*, one of the channel's most famous shows, "guests were known to enter screaming matches, spout insults and threats, and even storm off set."[13] Another popular program, *Religion and Life*, featured pronouncements by radical Egyptian cleric Yusuf al-Qaradawi, the so-called spiritual guide of Hamas. Qaradawi dispensed advice on topics "from the Arab Spring to female masturbation."[14]

Just two years after its inception, *Al-Jazeera* was crowned the "most influential Arab TV channel," and soon began to rival *CNN* in terms of prestige and reputation.[15] *Al-Jazeera* had the soft power effect Hamad intended. With satellite dishes now ubiquitous across the Middle East, the channel was celebrated worldwide as a tool to "undermine censorship in individual states and expand the bounds of freedom throughout the region."[16]

Success did not come cheaply, however. Upon *Al-Jazeera*'s inauguration, Hamad endowed it with initial funding of $140 million to subsidize operations until 2001, when it was expected to become self-sufficient from advertising profits. In 2002, however, the Qatari government was spending roughly $100 million annually to "sustain the network."[17] Though exact figures are hard to come by, since the network does not disclose finances, the Qatari royal family reportedly continues to fund *Al-Jazeera*.[18] The network is today a fully-owned subsidiary of the Qatar Media Corporation, which itself is owned by the Qatari royal family.[19]

In keeping with this arrangement, the network's top brass are members of the ruling family. Hamad bin Thamer al Thani, a relative of the *emir*, has been *Al-Jazeera*'s chairman since the channel's inception and he is also CEO of the Qatar Media Corporation. Bin Thamer was an under-secretary at the Ministry of Information, prior to its abolition, and was later appointed head of the General Authority for Qatari Radio and Television in 1997.[20] Qatari Radio and Television is responsible for overseeing all Qatari media, which includes several networks, among them *Al-Jazeera English*.[21]

Al-Jazeera has now grown to encompass more than ten channels, including the flagship Arabic news channel and its English-language sister, as well as *Al-Jazeera Mubasher*, *Al-Jazeera Documentary*, *Al-Jazeera Balkans*, and others.[22] The network launched an *Al-Jazeera America* in 2013 after purchasing the cable broadcast rights from former Vice President Al Gore's *Current TV*, but the venture ultimately folded in early 2016 due to poor ratings and miniscule viewership.[23]

Al-Jazeera Sport, for its part, has since become beIN Media Group, which the *New York Times* describes as a "major plank of Qatar's efforts... to brand itself as a global and regional power." BeIN Media has spent billions of dollars purchasing streaming rights to major soccer competitions – including the UEFA Champions League and England's Premier League – after Qatar was awarded rights to host the 2022 World Cup.[24]

Emir Hamad's son Tamim sees sports as the next frontier in Qatar's attempts to cultivate influence. Tamim is a sports enthusiast, but the push is strategic, given the huge market that the Middle East represents for sports broadcasting.

An Interconnected Network

Al-Jazeera is not the only outlet affiliated with Qatar, though its popularity and scope far exceed the rest. Qatar is purported to fund *Al-Araby al-Jadeed* (The New Arab) and *Middle East Eye*, which publish in English and Arabic, in addition to the Arabic-only *HuffPost Arabi*.

Reuters reported that Qatar launched *Al-Araby al-Jadeed* in 2015.[25] The outlet's creator and editor-in-chief is Azmi Bishara, a former Israeli Knesset member now based in Doha.[26] Bishara is a key advisor to the current *emir* and head of a government-supported think tank.

UAE newspaper *The National* first disclosed a connection between *Middle East Eye* (MEE) and Qatar in 2014. An *Al-Jazeera* employee served as a launch consultant for MEE briefly before returning to work on special projects for *Al-Jazeera*'s chairman's office.[27] MEE's website says it is operated by "M.E.E. Ltd.," and British corporate filings show that Jamal Awn Jamal Bessasso is the only person with significant control in both *Middle East Eye* and M.E.E. Ltd.[28] According to *The National*, Bessasso was "a director of planning and human resources" at *Al-Jazeera* and an ex-director for *Samalink TV*, "the registered agent for the website of the Hamas-controlled *al-Quds TV*."[29]

Qatar also had extensive ties to *HuffPost Arabi*, which launched in July 2015 as a joint venture between the *Huffington Post* and Integral Media Strategies, the company of former *Al-Jazeera* managing director Waddah Khanfar.[30] As scholar Michael Rubin notes, despite taking on the progressive brand of *Huffington Post*, *HuffPost Arabi* was anything but. The outlet became renowned for running perspectives espoused by Islamists, promoting the "Muslim Brotherhood, anti-Semitism, sectarian strife, anti-gay bias, and more."[31]

In turn, *HuffPost Arabi* had the ability to cross-post to a host of other *Al-Jazeera*-affiliated media outlets, including *Middle East Eye*, *Noon Post*, the Tunisian Press Agency, Turk Press, *Sasa Post*, and *Libya Al-Khabar*. With the exception of *Sasa Post*, Rubin found that all these outlets were registered to *Al Jazeera Turk*'s media director.[32] *HuffPost Arabi* ceased operations as of late March 2018, without providing a reason.[33]

THE DOMESTIC LANDSCAPE

While the Qatari government pushed the boundaries of Arab media across the region, the emirate considerably less ambitious at home. Seven newspapers, published in either English or Arabic, are all under the direct ownership of the ruling family or controlled by a close associate.[34] Broadcast choices are even more limited; there are only two domestic television networks in the country: *Qatar TV* and *Al-Jazeera*. *Qatar TV* focuses on official news and offers pro-government perspectives, while *Al-Jazeera* covers global and regional news that rarely, if ever, touch on Qatari politics at home.

Officially, Qatar has no formal censorship: Emir Hamad in 1995 abolished the Ministry of Information, which oversaw censorship, and replaced it with the General Association for Qatari Radio and Television (headed by *Al-Jazeera* chairman Hamad bin Thamer).[35] But a variety of topics constitute red lines in the emirate, including criticism of the government or royal family, migrant workers' rights, and Islam.[36]

A press and publications law enacted in 1979, as well as broadly framed antiterrorism legislation, are both invoked to censor content. Additionally, a cybercrime law penalizes the distribution of "false news," a violation of "social values or principles," or any "online behavior that can jeopardize state security," with up to a three-year prison term and a fine of up to $137,000. Online defamation is also punishable by a one-year prison term or a fine of up $27,000.[37]

Additionally, authorities block certain websites without clear justification, as was the case with the English-language *Doha News*. The outlet, according to Freedom House, "had a history of covering sensitive or controversial issues omitted by most local news providers."[38] For example, in August 2016, *Doha News* published an editorial where a young Qatari, under a pseudonym, discussed life in Qatar as a gay man; same-sex sexual activity remains illegal in Qatar, and *Doha News*' publication stirred major controversy. Earlier, in July 2016, security forces detained assistant editor Peter Kovessy for his reporting on a child sexual abuse case, although the case was quickly dropped.[39] In November 2016, authorities blocked the website but did not say why. Though it is now accessible, its content is significantly less edgy.

As Mohammed Arafa, the former chairman of Qatar University's communications department, observed in 2002: "Legally, the press has not a leg to stand on in Qatar, which is very unusual for a country launching a free twenty-four-hour news channel."[40] More than a decade-and-a-half after Arafa's assessment, nothing has changed in this regard.

Lastly, self-censorship is widespread, particularly among foreign journalists. All foreign journalists in Qatar must receive accreditation from the Foreign Information Agency. Citizenship requirements make it impossible for foreigners to obtain media licenses. When their coverage is deemed impermissible, non-Qataris face much tougher punishments, including "termination, deportation, and imprisonment." Even professionals in compliance with the rules can be harassed, arrested, or denied entry into Qatar.[41]

Qatari citizens are not blind to the double standards. As authors Mohammed El-Nawawy and Adel Iskandar note, "they have a real taste of freedom of expression, but when it comes to local issues they see nothing but tiresome government public relations."[42]

A TOOL OF FOREIGN POLICY

But even that freedom of expression has faded in recent years. Increasingly, *Al-Jazeera* hews more closely to Doha's foreign policies.[43] This appears to be a deliberate decision. Leaked diplomatic cables from 2009 reveal Qatari officials boasting about altering *Al-Jazeera*'s coverage to buttress their foreign policy.[44]

Saudi Arabia

From its early days, *Al-Jazeera* was intentionally anti-Saudi, stemming from Hamad's belief that the Kingdom sponsored a counter-coup against him. The channel gave "special attention" to criticizing Saudi Arabia and well as Egypt, both of which had disapproved of Hamad's power grab.[45] By 2002, tensions over *Al-Jazeera* got so bad that Saudi Arabia broke ties with Qatar and recalled its ambassador from Doha. The Kingdom chafed at *Al-Jazeera*'s airing of a panel discussion with Saudi dissidents, while also giving unfavorable coverage of the Kingdom's proposed peace plan for the Israeli-Palestinian conflict.[46] The dispute was only resolved in 2008, when *Al-Jazeera* softened its Saudi reporting – a move widely viewed as a "prelude to Saudi-Qatari rapprochement."[47]

Whatever goodwill was established as a result, however, evaporated in 2014 when Saudi Arabia, the UAE, and Bahrain withdrew their ambassadors from Doha in protest over Qatari meddling in countries impacted by the Arab Spring. Tensions eased again until 2017, when Saudi Arabia joined in a regional blockade of Qatar – once again, an expression of broad frustration with Qatari policies. The Saudis, along with the UAE, Bahrain, and Egypt, issued a list of demands Qatar would be required to meet in order to end the blockade. Shuttering *Al-Jazeera*, Qatar's most effective tool for fomenting unrest and rallying Islamists to challenge the regional status quo, was among them.

The Israeli-Palestinian conflict

The second *intifada*, which erupted in 2000, was the moment that made *Al-Jazeera* a household name. During the violent campaign that marked the death of the Oslo Peace Process, author Hugh Miles notes, the channel "became a forum for those involved in the uprising and a window for those outside."[48] According to celebrated Arab scholar Fouad Ajami, *Al-Jazeera*'s reporting "barely feigned neutrality."[49] *Al-Jazeera* used its power to mobilize support for Palestinian violence while diminishing the negative impact, including the inevitable despair deriving from the end of peace talks.

Two days after the *intifada* started, an *Al-Jazeera* news crew grabbed footage of Israeli soldiers shooting a twelve-year-old Palestinian boy, Mohammed al-Durra, and repeatedly played the clip of the boy's death. For days, "the picture of his dying became the network's emblem of the intifada."[50] Even some Palestinians expressed concern at the way the channel replayed the images in an opportunistic manner.[51] Israel disputes the veracity of the al-Durra saga, claiming the entire thing was staged.[52]

Whether or not *Al-Jazeera* staged the shooting is almost inconsequential. The network stirred the emotions of its Arab audience by other means as well. The network referred to Palestinian dead as *shahid*, the Arabic word for martyrs. *Al-Jazeera* applied this term to Palestinian suicide bombers as well–a less-than-subtle endorsement of the terrorist tactic.[53] Also, as the *New York Times* noted, there was a double standard. "Palestinians who fell to Israeli gunfire were martyrs," but "Israelis killed by Palestinians were Israelis killed by Palestinians."[54]

Al-Jazeera's *intifada* coverage had geopolitical consequences, too. Appearances by radical spokesmen on the channel, such as Hezbollah's Hassan Nasrallah, "made it increasingly difficult for Egypt to stick to a moderate course" regarding its diplomatic ties to Israel. In the end, amid the furor stoked by *Al-Jazeera* in Egypt, Mubarak recalled the Egyptian ambassador to Israel, reportedly saying, "I had to do something." As the *intifada* wore on, *Al-Jazeera* began using the word *khawana*, meaning traitors, to attack Egypt's "soft stance" against Israel.[55]

Even among other spates of Palestinian unrest in recent years, *Al-Jazeera* has remained a strident proponent of the Palestinian cause, tacitly endorsing knife and vehicular attacks, or other acts of violence.[56]

Bin Laden tapes

If the second *intifada* made *Al-Jazeera* famous, it was Osama bin Laden who made the network infamous. For the Qatari network's viewers, bin Laden was not an arch terrorist. Rather, he was a "gun-wielding millionaire turned into a legend by the West."[57] At least, that is how the network described him shortly after September 11, 2001, when it re-ran an exclusive interview it had taped with the al-Qaeda chief in 1998.

In the aftermath of the 9/11 attacks, *Al-Jazeera* was the only broadcaster to obtain exclusive interviews and taped messages from Osama bin Laden. His reliance on *Al-Jazeera* to disseminate his message–and *Al-Jazeera*'s apparent willingness to oblige him–raised troubling questions as to whether the network was coordinating with al-Qaeda. Bin Laden had sent tapes to other Arab networks before, but they ignored his videos given the obvious dangers. Not so with *Al-Jazeera*, which aired his messages so often it was soon dubbed "Bin Laden TV" by some in the foreign press. It was particularly hard to shake this image after the network's correspondent, Ahmad Zaydan, was the only journalist present at the wedding of bin Laden's son in Afghanistan in January 2001.[58] A decade later, the network's Afghanistan correspondent, Taysir Alluni, was found guilty by a Spanish court of being a major financier for al-Qaeda – a charge both he and the network vehemently denied.[59]

In their exhaustive portrait of bin Laden in exile, Cathy Scott-Clark and Adrian Levy note that *Al-Jazeera* was the al-Qaeda leader's "favorite outlet." Even when he was on the run and likely injured, bin Laden used the network to demonstrate to his followers that he was "still alive and committed to global jihad," the authors note.[60] In a letter to bin Laden, al-Qaeda senior leader Atiyah Abd al-Rahman discussed working with *Al-Jazeera* to produce a documentary on bin Laden, saying he would "send the idea to Zidan."[61] The name most likely refers to *Al-Jazeera* journalist Ahmad Zaydan, who attended bin Laden's son's wedding.

Al-Jazeera's amplification of bin Laden's message did not sit well with U.S. policymakers. In October 2001, then-Secretary of State Colin Powell lodged a formal complaint with Emir Hamad, asking him to "rein in" the channel. Hamad rebuffed Powell, however, insisting on the need for "free and reliable media."[62] When the Pentagon struck *Al-Jazeera*'s Kabul bureau in November 2001, the network was quick to accuse the George W. Bush administration of doing so deliberately.[63] Intentional or not, there was growing anger in policy-making circles over *Al-Jazeera*'s perceived role in supporting terrorist violence – anger which would only intensify during the subsequent Iraq war.

Iraq war

Al-Jazeera's strident anti-American rhetoric and the perception that it was fanning the flames of anti-American violence in Iraq almost made the channel a recipient of an intentional Pentagon strike, according to a leaked memo attributed to former President George W. Bush. The memo, which some former officials now openly question, alleges that Bush considered bombing the network's headquarters in Doha during the 2004 insurgency in Falluja.[64]

From the war's onset, *Al-Jazeera* was unabashedly anti-American in its coverage. While other networks referred to Saddam Hussein as Iraq's dictator, *Al-Jazeera* called him its president. Coalition troops were "invasion forces," while Iraqi forces were the "resistance" – terminology adopted as early as the war's third day.[65] Suicide bombings were "commando attacks," or even "paradise operations."[66] The war on terror became the "so-called War on Terror" in *Al-Jazeera*'s parlance.[67] As analyst Hussein Ibish observed, the entire war was "portrayed virtually as a campaign of mass murder."[68] In one instance, the network aired a report about an old Iraqi who recounted shooting down an Apache helicopter with a hunting rifle near Karbala. The entire piece, notes Hugh Miles, "smelt strongly of Iraqi propaganda trying to shame the local tribesmen into resisting the advancing coalition."[69]

The network opposed the United States in other ways as well. It aired clips of captured American soldiers and clips of several dead American and British service members, without obscuring their faces. Enraged, the Pentagon pressured the network to hold the footage for eight hours, so authorities could inform the families of the dead. While the network brass agreed to the Pentagon's request, *Al-Jazeera*'s website ran the footage online anyway.[70]

What concerned U.S. policymakers the most, though, was the possibility that *Al-Jazeera* was actually working directly with the insurgency. Former Defense Secretary Donald Rumsfeld lambasted the station, noting that it had found itself "in very close proximity to things that were happening against coalition forces before the event happened and during the event."[71] At a Pentagon briefing in 2003, Rumsfeld accused the network of working with insurgents in filming and broadcasting attacks against coalition forces.[72] The former head of U.S. Central Command, Gen. John Abizaid, echoed that sentiment and wondered how "Al-Jazeera always manages to be at the scene of the crime or when a hostage shows up."[73]

The irony of *Al-Jazeera*'s coverage is that Qatar was simultaneously serving as the nerve center for America's Iraq operations. While U.S. soldiers were fighting the war out of the al-Udeid air base, *Al-Jazeera*, only a short drive away, was broadcasting the words of Yousef al-Qaradawi, who professed at the war's onset in 2003 that Muslims who attack the American presence were "carrying the spirit of true defenders," and would die as martyrs. Qaradawi also asserted that "Americans in Iraq are all fighters and invaders" and implored Muslims to believe that "fighting American civilians in Iraq is a duty for all Muslims."[74]

Some argued that the rhetoric was a useful for Doha's rulers, conveying the image that "they are not in bed with the United States."[75] But *Al-Jazeera*'s vitriol, which fanned the flames of Iraqi frustrations as U.S. operations wore on, greatly complicated the coalition's efforts in Iraq.

The Arab Spring

Much ink has been spilled on the significance of the role played by *Al-Jazeera* in amplifying the voices of the protestors during the course of the Arab Spring.[76] Yet, in spite of whatever positive role the network may have played, history will not be kind to the Qataris. Their television station quickly came to be seen as a tool that advanced a pro-Muslim

Brotherhood foreign policy at the expense of balanced reporting.

Adel Iskandar, the author of a book on *Al-Jazeera*, notes that while the network had once "had a firewall between its governmental funding and its broadcast content," that barrier broke down as the popular unrest in the region wore on.[77] Signs that the network was deliberately backing the Brotherhood were evident when Egyptians began protesting in the streets against Muslim Brotherhood rule in early 2013. *Al-Jazeera* was critical of those protestors in what appeared to be an attempt to dissuade them from taking to the streets. This, of course, reflected the political leanings of the government in Doha.[78]

Indeed, from the Arab Spring's early days, *Al-Jazeera* amplified Islamist perspectives. It hosted Rachid Ghannouchi, founder of Tunisia's Muslim Brotherhood-linked Ennahda party, whose past appearances on the channel actually led Tunis to recall its ambassador to Qatar. In an interview given after Tunisia's uprising, Ghannouchi called Qatar a "partner" in Tunisia's revolution, citing *Al-Jazeera*'s favorable coverage of Ennahda.[79] In 2016, Ghannouchi thanked *Al-Jazeera* for "support we have got from it," claiming that "*Al-Jazeera* introduced our case, revolution and its figures to the world."[80] *Al-Jazeera*'s think tank, the Al Jazeera Center for Studies, even released Ghannouchi's book in October 2012 – a month after holding a symposium featuring Ghannouchi and Hassan Turabi, the Sudanese Islamist who previously sheltered bin Laden.[81]

But the summer of 2013, when the Egyptian army ousted Mohammed Morsi, the country's Muslim Brotherhood president, was the real tipping point, notes former *Al-Jazeera English* employee Gregg Carlstrom.[82] The network effectively became the mouthpiece for Morsi. The *Al-Jazeera Mubasher Misr* channel devolved into an outlet whose goal was to present "local news with a clear pro-Brotherhood bias." The *Al-Jazeera* website featured pieces similar in tone. In late 2013, one article decried "the war that was waged against [Morsi] in other media outlets." With the headline "Morsi's economic successes and the coup government's failure," the article did not even feign objectivity.[83]

Unsurprisingly, Qaradawi used his position on *Al-Jazeera* to incite protestors in defense of the Brotherhood. In August 2013, during Egypt's military crackdown on the group, he gave a long speech on *Al-Jazeera* demanding Egyptians take to the streets against the army. Calling it a religious obligation for "every able-bodied" Egyptian, he claimed the government was "complicit in these massacres" and would "answer to Allah."[84] He issued a similar call around that time to Sunnis in Syria to mobilize against Syrian President Bashar al Assad, warning that Hezbollah and

Shia Muslims would "devour" them.[85]

Failure to toe this line reportedly came at a price for some employees of *Al-Jazeera*. When one reporter asked a Brotherhood spokesperson at a pro-Morsi sit-in why women and children were present if they might be targeted by the Egyptian military, she was pulled off the air and "reprimanded for being insufficiently sympathetic to the group," and "relegated to a pre-recorded chat show."[86]

The Cairo bureau chief of *Al-Jazeera English*, Mohammed Fahmy, also learned some tough lessons about his employers. He had signed on with *Al-Jazeera* on the condition that *Al-Jazeera English*'s work never air on its Arabic-language sister, to preserve the integrity of its work. Doha management agreed. And yet, one day, Fahmy caught a video package he had produced about teenagers detained in adult prisons airing on the pro-Brotherhood *Al-Jazeera Mubasher Misr*. Nor was this the only instance of his work appearing on *Mubasher Misr*, which had been shuttered in Egypt but continued its broadcast illegally and covertly from *Al-Jazeera*'s Doha headquarters via a different satellite frequency.[87]

Fahmy was arrested in late 2013, and later sentenced to a 438-day prison term on sham charges of terrorism. He discovered that *Al-Jazeera* violated journalistic standards and played havoc with the security of its Egypt employees to pursue its pro-Brotherhood coverage. Remarkably, *Al-Jazeera* had lost its license to operate in Egypt two days after having hired Fahmy. The network's management hid this most important fact from its staff for over three months.[88]

Pro-Brotherhood actors in Libya and Syria enjoyed the same *Al-Jazeera* treatment. Ali Hashem, a former *Al-Jazeera* employee, resigned from the network in protest of the channel's "bias and whitewashing" of the revolution in Syria.[89] Hashem claimed he captured footage in 2011 of dozens of armed gunmen inside Syria, some possessing Kalashnikovs and rocket-propelled grenades.[90] *Al-Jazeera* refused to broadcast the footage for fear that it would convey the impression that the Syrian uprising was "becoming militarized." Hashem's orders were to bury the footage, since it "didn't fit the narrative of a clean and peaceful uprising."[91] Such orders telegraphed a "deliberate support of Qatar's anti-Assad stance and its narrative of a civil uprising."[92]

Ghassan Ben Jeddo, *Al-Jazeera*'s former Beirut bureau chief, resigned for similar reasons in April 2011, accusing the station of "completely abandoning objectivity and professionalism" and becoming instead "an operations room for incitement and mobilization."[93] Ahmed Mansour, presenter of the popular *Al-Jazeera* show "Without Limits," even went to Syria and interviewed Abu Muhammad al-Julani, leader of the Al Qaeda-affiliated Nusra Front extremist group. Controversially, Mansour stated that there is no difference between the Muslim Brotherhood and al-Qaeda.[94]

When NATO forces began their operations in Libya to overthrow the regime of Muammar al-Gaddafi, *Al-Jazeera* threw its weight behind the intervention, which presented another opportunity to overturn the existing order and aid the rise of Islamist rule. The network's double standard became instantly apparent. As journalists Roula Khalaf and Abeer Allam note, *Al-Jazeera* "highlighted the wars in Afghanistan and Iraq as American aggression against Muslims, but in the case of Libya... supported the revolution."[95]

Hamas

Qatar is conspicuous in its political and economic support of another Islamist group as well: the Palestinian terrorist organization Hamas. When Emir Hamad visited Gaza in 2012, he pledged $400 million in Qatari support to the group.[96] While Doha today says that it no longer finances the group, Emir Tamim is known to have pledged an additional $100 million as recently as 2017.[97] And in 2018, Tamim was the first world leader to call Hamas leader Ismail Haniyeh, just days after the U.S. Treasury Department placed him on its terrorist blacklist.[98] Hamas' former political chief, Khaled Meshaal, along with many other Hamas figures, has called Doha home since 2012.

Given Doha's strong support for Hamas, coupled with its favorable coverage of Palestinian unrest, it should come as no surprise that Hamas enjoys favorable *Al-Jazeera* coverage. When a new round of Israeli-Palestinian violence erupted in 2014, the network's reporting lacked any semblance of balance. According to Gulf scholar David Weinberg, the network followed guidelines released by Hamas' Interior Ministry on how to report the events in Gaza.[99] In one particularly egregious instance of flawed reporting, *Al-Jazeera* repeated Hamas allegations that Israel had attacked a UN school, without even a cursory mention that the Israeli Defense Forces denied intentionally targeting the school. When another school came under fire on July 30th of that year, *Al-Jazeera* repeated the same allegation and again omitted the IDF's denial.[100]

Several times, *Al-Jazeera* rearranged its primetime programs to air speeches for Hamas officials, including Meshaal and Mohammed Deif, the commander of Hamas' military wing. After airing Deif's message, *Al-Jazeera* showed a Hamas paramilitary propaganda video. On the last day of the conflict, *Al-Jazeera* once more altered its primetime schedule to broadcast an uninterrupted live news conference with Ramadan Shallah, secretary general of the Palestinian Islamic Jihad, an Iranian-backed terrorist group.[101]

When asked whether *Al-Jazeera* supports extremism, senior officials deftly sidestep the question. Doha's official line is that Hamas, while a terror group in the eyes of the U.S., is a "legitimate resistance movement" in the Arab world.[102] Another common refrain is that *Al-Jazeera* supports the Palestinian people, not Hamas – something Doha repeats officially as well.[103]

Al Jazeera's acting director general, Mostefa Souag, denies that the network gives a platform to extremists, but with a caveat. According to him, "90 percent of our audience are Muslims and they need to hear from these people," meaning Islamists.[104] As scholars David Weinberg, Grant Rumley, and Oren Adaki have noted, this pro-Hamas "partisanship" directly incites violence and feeds "the one-sided narrative of Palestinian victimhood" while boosting the standing of terror groups.[105] Hugh Miles, author of a book on the channel, adds that the network's reporting on the conflict has "probably made peace and reconciliation between Palestinians and Israelis more elusive."[106]

The Plan Backfires

Qatar's backing for Islamist organizations is partly ideological, with former *emir* Hamad said to enjoy an "infamously close" bond with Qaradawi.[107] But it reflects a deeper calculus as well. As Brotherhood-affiliated organizations swept the region during the Arab Spring, the movement "appeared to be the political wave of the future," scholar Eric Trager observed.[108] Supporting these groups was designed to give Doha more clout on the world stage. It constituted a low-risk, low-cost strategy for Qatar. Moreover, as the Qatari-backed *Middle East Eye* has suggested, the emirate supported Islamist movements in a conscious effort to differentiate itself from Saudi Arabia, especially in light of Qatar's "subservience to Saudi Arabia" during Khalifa bin Hamad's rule.[109]

But Qatar took things too far, according to its Gulf neighbors. To Saudi Arabia and the UAE, in particular, the rise of the Muslim Brotherhood across the region foreshadowed the possibility of a revival of their own domestic Brotherhood movements.[110] Qatar became a victim of these fears, earning the ire of its neighbors for being a "meddler that fueled division and empowered Islamists."[111] Ultimately, that acrimony pushed Saudi Arabia, the UAE, Bahrain, and Egypt to sever ties with Qatar in 2017. An economic blockade on Qatar imposed by those countries remains in force as of this writing.

As of May 2018, Qatar was on a charm offensive in Washington, eager to make new friends and thereby ease its international isolation. But Doha has achieved the opposite result following recent revelations that *Al-Jazeera* spied on purported pro-Israel organizations in Washington in order to produce a documentary.[112] The episode sparked outrage on Capitol Hill, with legislators seeking to force the network to register under the *U.S. Foreign Agents Registration Act* (FARA), which would end its image of independence.[113] Already, video platform YouTube includes a disclaimer that *Al-Jazeera* is Qatari-funded in videos posted by the network's YouTube channel.[114]

After visiting the Doha headquarters of *Al-Jazeera* back in the year 2000, former Egyptian president Hosni Mubarak is said to have scoffed: "all that noise from this little matchbox?" Eighteen years on, however, that "matchbox" still seems capable of roiling the region as a weaponized source of information and influence. Whether or not *Al-Jazeera* ultimately returns to its original mission of unbiased news reporting, depends entirely on its owners in Qatar.

ENDNOTES

1. David B. Roberts, "Securing the Qatari State," The Arab Gulf States Institute in Washington, June 23, 2017, http://www.agsiw.org/wp-content/uploads/2017/06/Roberts_Qatar_ONLINE.pdf.
2. Ibid.
3. Louay Y. Bahry, "The New Arab Media Phenomenon: Qatar's Al-Jazeera," *Middle East Policy* VIII, no. 2, Summer 2001, http://www.mepc.org/journal/new-arab-media-phenomenon-qatars-al-jazeera.
4. Hugh Miles, *Al Jazeera: The Inside Story of the Arab News Channel that is Challenging the West* (New York: Grove Press, 2005), 15.
5. Bahry, "The New Arab Media Phenomenon: Qatar's Al-Jazeera."
6. Roberts, "Securing the Qatari State."
7. Mohammed El Nawawy and Adel Iskandar, *Al Jazeera: How the Free Arab News Network Scooped the World and Changed the Middle East* (Cambridge: Westview Press, 2002), 32.
8. Bahry, "The New Arab Media Phenomenon: Qatar's Al-Jazeera."
9. Miles, *Al Jazeera: The Inside Story of the Arab News Channel that is Challenging the West*, 37.
10. Jon B. Alterman, *New Media, New Politics? From Satellite Television to the Internet in the Arab World*, (Washington: The Washington Institute, 1998), 16.
11. Miles, *Al Jazeera: The Inside Story of the Arab News Channel that is Challenging the West*, 93.
12. Ibid., 93.
13. Ibidem, 39.
14. Sudarsan Raghavan and Joby Warrick, "How a 91-year-old imam came to symbolize the feud between Qatar and its neighbors," *Washington Post*, June 27, 2017, https://www.washingtonpost.com/world/middle_east/how-a-91-year-old-imam-came-to-symbolize-feud-between-qatar-and-its-neighbors/2017/06/26/601d41b4-5157-11e7-91eb-9611861a988f_story.html?utm_term=.0a82975c2c21.
15. Bahry, "The New Arab Media Phenomenon: Qatar's Al-Jazeera."
16. Alterman, *New Media, New Politics?* 24.
17. El Nawawy and Iskandar, *Al Jazeera*, 33-34.
18. "Al Jazeera America closure marks a quieter Qatar," Reuters, January 27, 2016, https://www.reuters.com/article/qatar-power-al-jazeera/al-jazeera-america-closure-marks-a-quieter-qatar-idUSL8N1510U1

19. "Al Jazeera Media Network," *PrivCo*, n.d. (accessed April 30, 2018), https://www.privco.com/private-company/al-jazeera.

20. "Sheikh Hamad bin Thamer Al Thani," *Al-Jazeera* (Qatar), n.d. (accessed April 30, 2018), https://network.aljazeera.com/about-us/management-profiles/sheikh-hamad-bin-thamer-al-thani.

21. El Nawawy and Iskandar, *Al Jazeera*, 88.

22. "Who we are," *Al-Jazeera* (Qatar), n.d. (accessed May 1, 2018), https://www.aljazeera.com/aboutus/.

23. "Al Jazeera America closure marks a quieter Qatar."

24. Tariq Panja, "For Qatari Network beIN Sports, Political Feud Spills Into Stadiums," *New York Times*, September 11, 2017, https://www.nytimes.com/2017/09/11/sports/soccer/saudi-arabia-qatar-bein-sports.html.

25. "Al Jazeera America closure marks a quieter Qatar."

26. David Roberts, "Qatar and the Muslim Brotherhood: Pragmatism or Preference?" *Middle East Policy* XXI, no. 3, Fall 2014, http://www.mepc.org/qatar-and-muslim-brotherhood-pragmatism-or-preference.

27. James Langton, "New London connection to Islamists," *The National* (UAE), June 26, 2014, https://www.thenational.ae/uae/new-london-connection-to-islamists-1.648408.

28. Middle East Eye, "Terms of website use," n.d. (accessed May 2, 2018), http://www.middleeasteye.net/terms-and-conditions; Companies House, Corporate Filing, "Middle East Eye Limited," Number 09814915 (accessed May 2, 2018), https://beta.companieshouse.gov.uk/company/09814915/persons-with-significant-control; Companies House, Corporate Filing, M.E.E Limited, Number 08803692 (accessed May 2, 2018), https://beta.companieshouse.gov.uk/company/08803692/persons-with-significant-control.

29. Langton, "New London connection to Islamists."

30. Tom Gara, "A Stand Against Atheists, Gays, and Selfies," *Buzzfeed*, August 9, 2015, https://www.buzzfeed.com/tomgara/huffington-post-takes-a-stand-against-selfies?fb_comment_id=855367107880355_855428127874253&comment_id=855428127874253&offset=0&total_comments=11&utm_term=.eyd5vxEAg#.ueYBkJNEn.

31. Michael Rubin, "Why is Huffington Promoting Muslim Brotherhood Media?" *Commentary*, August 21, 2015, https://www.commentarymagazine.com/foreign-policy/middle-east/arianna-huff-

ington-muslim-brotherhood-media/.

32. Ibid.
33. Mina Aldroubi, "Huffington Post shuts down its Arabic services," *The National* (UAE), April 2, 2018, https://www.thenational.ae/world/mena/huffington-post-shuts-down-its-arabic-services-1.718138.
34. Freedom House, "Freedom of the Press 2017: Qatar," 2017 (accessed April 30, 2018), https://freedomhouse.org/report/freedom-press/2017/qatar.
35. El Nawawy and Iskandar, *Al Jazeera*, 37.
36. Reporters Without Borders, "Qatar," n.d. (accessed April 30, 2018), https://rsf.org/en/qatar.
37. Freedom House, "Freedom of the Press 2017: Qatar."
38. Ibid.
39. Ibidem.
40. El Nawawy and Iskandar, *Al Jazeera*, 88.
41. Freedom House, "Freedom of the Press 2017: Qatar."
42. El Nawawy and Iskandar, *Al Jazeera*, 85.
43. Simon Henderson, "The 'al-Jazeera Effect': Arab Satellite Television and Public Opinion," Washington Institute for Near East Policy *PolicyWatch* no. 507, December 8, 2000, http://www.washingtoninstitute.org/policy-analysis/view/the-al-jazeera-effect-arab-satellite-television-and-public-opinion.
44. Robert Booth, "WikiLeaks cables claim al-Jazeera changed coverage to suit Qatari foreign policy," *Guardian* (London), December 5, 2010, https://www.theguardian.com/world/2010/dec/05/wikileaks-cables-al-jazeera-qatari-foreign-policy.
45. Henderson, "The 'al-Jazeera Effect.'"
46. Gregg Carlstrom, "What's the Problem with Al Jazeera?" *The Atlantic*, June 24, 2017, https://www.theatlantic.com/international/archive/2017/06/al-jazeera-qatar-saudi-arabia-muslim-brotherhood/531471/; Kevin Ponniah, "Qatar crisis: Can Al Jazeera survive?" *BBC News*, June 8, 2017, http://www.bbc.com/news/world-middle-east-40187414.
47. "Saudi ambassador returns to Qatar after 5-yr gap," Reuters, March 9, 2008, https://www.reuters.com/article/saudi-qatar/saudi-ambassador-returns-to-qatar-after-5-yr-gap-idUSL0925349720080309.
48. Miles, *Al Jazeera*, 68.
49. Fouad Ajami, "What the Muslim World is Watching," *The New*

York Times Magazine, November 18, 2001, https://www.nytimes.com/2001/11/18/magazine/what-the-muslim-world-is-watching.html.
50. Miles, *Al Jazeera*, 73.
51. Ajami, "What the Muslim World is Watching."
52. Alistair Dawber, "The killing of 12-year-old Mohammed al-Durrah in Gaza became the defining image of the second intifada. Only Israel claims it was all a fake," *Independent* (London), May 20, 2013, https://www.independent.co.uk/news/world/middle-east/the-killing-of-12-year-old-mohammed-al-durrah-in-gaza-became-the-defining-image-of-the-second-8624311.html.
53. El Nawawy and Iskandar, *Al Jazeera*, 52.
54. Ajami, "What the Muslim World is Watching."
55. Miles, *Al Jazeera*, 83-86.
56. @DavidAWeinberg, "'Martyrdom.' How #AlJazeera describes killing of man near Hebron allegedly trying to drive over IDF troops: Aljazeera.net/news/Arabic/20," *Twitter*, July 18, 2017, https://twitter.com/DavidAWeinberg/status/887388952927367171.
57. Miles, *Al Jazeera*, 110.
58. Ibidem, 109-112.
59. "Freed Al Jazeera journalist returns to Doha," *Al-Jazeera* (Qatar), March 12, 2012, https://www.aljazeera.com/news/middleeast/2012/03/201231214310717459.html.
60. Cathy Scott-Clark and Adrian Levy, *The Exile: The Stunning Inside Story of Osama bin Laden and al Qaeda in Flight* (London: Bloomsbury, 2017), 19, 89.
61. Mahmud letter to Sheikh Abu-' Abdallah (accessed May 1, 2018), https://www.longwarjournal.org/wp-content/uploads/2015/03/EXHIBIT-423-ENG-TRANS-EX-422-56202CC8-.pdf.
62. "US urges curb on Arab TV channel," *BBC News*, October 4, 2001, http://news.bbc.co.uk/2/hi/americas/1578619.stm.
63. Matt Wells, "Al-Jazeera accuses US of bombing its Kabul office," *Guardian* (London), November 17, 2001, https://www.theguardian.com/media/2001/nov/17/warinafghanistan2001.afghanistan.
64. Dominic Timms, "Al-Jazeera seeks answers over 'bombing' memo," *Guardian* (London), November 23, 2005, https://www.theguardian.com/media/2005/nov/23/iraq.iraqandthemedia.
65. Miles, *Al Jazeera*, 252-253.
66. Oren Kessler, "The Two Faces of Al Jazeera," *Middle East Quar-*

terly 19, no. 1, Winter 2012, https://www.meforum.org/articles/2012/the-two-faces-of-al-jazeera.

67. Miles, *Al Jazeera*, 351.

68. Hussein Ibish, "Why America Turned Off Al Jazeera," *New York Times*, February 17, 2016, https://www.nytimes.com/2016/02/18/opinion/why-america-turned-off-al-jazeera.html.

69. Miles, *Al Jazeera*, 252.

70. Ibid., 248-250.

71. "Rumsfeld blasts Arab TV stations," *BBC News*, November 26, 2003, http://news.bbc.co.uk/2/hi/middle_east/3238680.stm.

72. "U.S. Accuses Two Popular Arab Networks of Working with Iraqi Insurgents," *PBS Newshour*, November 26, 2003, https://www.pbs.org/newshour/nation/media-july-dec03-arab_networks_11-26.

73. As cited in Tal Samuel-Azran, *Al-Jazeera and US War Coverage* (New York: Peter Lang Publishing Inc., 2010), 87.

74. Andrew C. McCarthy, "The Bin Bayyah Bungle," *National Review*, June 29, 2013, https://www.nationalreview.com/2013/06/bin-bayyah-bungle-andrew-c-mccarthy/.

75. Miles, *Al Jazeera*, 351-352.

76. Robert F. Worth and David D. Kirkpatrick, "Seizing a Moment, Al Jazeera Galvanizes Arab Frustration," *New York Times,* January 27, 2011, https://www.nytimes.com/2011/01/28/world/middleeast/28jazeera.html.

77. Mohamed Elshinnawi, "Qatar's Activism Sparks a Backlash," *Voice of America*, January 17, 2014, https://www.voanews.com/a/qatars-activism-sparks-a-backlash/1832277.html.

78. Alexander Kuhn, Cristoph Reuter, and Gregor Peter Schmitz, "Al-Jazeera Losing Battle for Independence," *Der Spiegel* (Berlin), February 15, 2013, http://www.spiegel.de/international/world/al-jazeera-criticized-for-lack-of-independence-after-arab-spring-a-883343.html.

79. Roberts, "Qatar and the Muslim Brotherhood: Pragmatism or Preference?"

80. Mohammed Osman, "Qatar partner in Tunisia's democratic transition, says Rachid Ghannouchi of Ennahda," *The Peninsula* (Doha), December 3, 2016, https://www.thepeninsulaqatar.com/article/03/12/2016/Qatar-partner-in-Tunisia-s-democratic-transition,-says-Rached-Ghannouchi-of-Ennahda.

81. Larbi Sadiki, "Tunisia: 'Ghannouchi for president?'" *Al-Jazeera*

(Doha), October 11, 2012, https://www.aljazeera.com/indepth/opinion/2012/10/2012101161016303637.html; "Hassan al-Turabi, Sudan opposition leader who hosted Osama bin Laden, dies," Associated Press, March 5, 2016, https://www.theguardian.com/world/2016/mar/06/hassan-al-turabi-sudan-opposition-leader-who-hosted-osama-bin-laden-dies.

82. Gregg Carlstrom, "What's the Problem with Al Jazeera?" *The Atlantic*, June 24, 2017, https://www.theatlantic.com/international/archive/2017/06/al-jazeera-qatar-saudi-arabia-muslim-brotherhood/531471/.

83. "إنجازات مرسي الاقتصادية وفشل حكومة الانقلاب" (Morsi's economic successes and the failure of the coup government)," *Al-Jazeera* (Qatar), September 10, 2013, http://www.aljazeera.net/news/ebusiness/2013/9/10/إنجازات-مرسي-الاقتصادية-وفشل-حكومة-الانقلاب.

84. David Schenker, "Qaradawi's War for Egypt," *The Majalla*, November 21, 2013, http://www.washingtoninstitute.org/policy-analysis/view/qaradawis-war-for-egypt.

85. "Syria conflict: Cleric Qaradawi urges Sunnis to join rebels," *BBC News*, June 1, 2013, http://www.bbc.com/news/world-middle-east-22741588.

86. Carlstrom, "What's the Problem with Al Jazeera?"

87. Mohamed Fahmy, *The Marriott Cell: An Epic Journey from Cairo's Scorpion Prison to Freedom* (Canada: Random House Canada, 2016), 122-124.

88. Ibid., 347-348.

89. Ibidem, 334.

90. Ibidem.

91. Ali Hashem, "The Arab spring has shaken Arab TV's credibility," *Guardian* (London), April 3, 2012, https://www.theguardian.com/commentisfree/2012/apr/03/arab-spring-arab-tv-credibility.

92. Fahmy, *The Marriott Cell*, 334.

93. Ali Ajmi, "غسان بن جدو يستقيل من قناة الجزيرة" (Ghassan ben Jeddo resigns from Al-Jazeera)," *Elaph* (Saudi Arabia), April 23, 2011, http://elaph.com/Web/arts/2011/4/649131.html.

94. Al Jazeera Arabic, "بلا حدود-أبو محمد الجولاني أمير جبهة النصرة" (Without Limits–Abu Muhammad al Julani, Emir of the Nusra Front)," *YouTube*, May 27, 2015, https://www.youtube.com/watch?v=-hwQT43vFZA.

95. Roula Khalaf and Abeer Allam, "Al-Jazeera's backing is key for co-

alition," *Financial Times*, March 20, 2011, https://www.ft.com/content/202f4b50-5312-11e0-86e6-00144feab49a.

96. Jodi Rudoren, "Qatar's Emir Visits Gaza, Pledging $400 Million to Hamas," *New York Times*, October 23, 2012, https://www.nytimes.com/2012/10/24/world/middleeast/pledging-400-million-qatari-emir-makes-historic-visit-to-gaza-strip.html.

97. Kate Harvard and Jonathan Schanzer, "By Hosting Hamas, Qatar is Whitewashing Terror," *Newsweek*, May 11, 2017, http://www.newsweek.com/qatar-hosting-hamas-whitewashing-terror-606750.

98. Khaled Abu Toameh, "Qatar leader promises Hamas emergency aid for struggling Gaza," *Times of Israel*, February 9, 2018, https://www.timesofisrael.com/qatar-leader-promises-hamas-emergency-aid-for-struggling-gaza/.

99. David Andrew Weinberg, Oren Adaki and Grant Rumley, "The Problem with Al Jazeera," *The National Interest*, September 10, 2014, http://nationalinterest.org/feature/the-problem-al-jazeera-11239?page=show.

100. Ibid.

101. Ibidem.

102. "Qatari FM insists Hamas 'a legitimate resistance movement,'" *Times of Israel*, June 10, 2017, https://www.timesofisrael.com/qatari-fm-insists-hamas-a-legitimate-resistance-movement/.

103. "فلسطين القطري بالدعم يشيد هنية (Haniyeh highlights Qatari support for Palestine)," *Al-Jazeera* (Doha), December 19, 2017, http://www.aljazeera.net/news/arabic/2017/12/19/هنية-يشيد-بالدعم-القطري-لفلسطين.

104. Mehdi Hasan, "Voice of the Arab Spring: Mehdi Hasan on Al Jazeera," *The New Statesman*, December 7, 2011, https://www.newstatesman.com/broadcast/2011/12/arab-channel-jazeera-qatar.

105. Weinberg, Adaki, and Rumley, "The Problem with Al Jazeera."

106. Miles, *Al Jazeera*, 368.

107. Eric Trager, "The Muslim Brotherhood Is the Root of the Qatar Crisis," *The Atlantic*, July 2, 2017, https://www.theatlantic.com/international/archive/2017/07/muslim-brotherhood-qatar/532380/.

108. Ibid.

109. Courtney Freer, "The Muslim Brotherhood and the GCC: It's complicated," *Middle East Eye*, July 3, 2017, http://www.middleeasteye.net/columns/muslim-brotherhood-and-gcc-it-s-complicat-

ed-510074443.

110. Trager, "The Muslim Brotherhood Is the Root of the Qatar Crisis."

111. Ibid.

112. Sue Surkes, "American pro-Israel lobby girds for Al Jazeera exposé," *Times of Israel*, February 8, 2018, https://www.timesofisrael.com/american-pro-israel-lobby-girds-for-al-jazeera-expose/. Disclosure: A conversation with one of the authors, Jonathan Schanzer, was among those recorded.

113. Josh Gerstein, "Lawmakers push for Al Jazeera to register as foreign agent," *Politico*, March 5, 2018, https://www.politico.com/story/2018/03/05/al-jazeera-press-foreign-agent-437072.

114. @DavidAWeinberg, "Thank you, @YouTube, for adding this important new disclaimer in the US below videos from #AlJazeera, stating that 'Al Jazeera is funded in whole or in part by the Qatari government.' Similar disclaimers being rolled out around the world, it seems," Twitter post, February 12, 2018, https://twitter.com/DavidAWeinberg/status/966373347389997056.

THE WORLD ACCORDING TO TEHRAN
David Denehy

Although it has received far less attention than other facets of its behavior, such as its nuclear program and persistent sponsorship of international terrorism, the Islamic Republic of Iran boasts an extensive and far-reaching media strategy. Within the country, Iranian authorities restrict free speech and intimidate opposition to the ruling regime. Abroad, the Iranian government has harnessed the media as a soft power tool to advance its foreign policy goals.

Iran's domestic media environment is profoundly constrained. The country ranks poorly on a multitude of press freedom indices (receiving a score of 90 out of 100 from Freedom House in 2017, and ranking 164th in the world the following year according to the estimates of Reporters without Borders).[1] This criticism is well deserved; despite the Iranian government's rhetoric about media freedom, journalists within the Islamic Republic live in fear of attack – whether it be arrest, prison, abuse or even, in some cases, death.

The Iranian regime's repressive approach to the media has historical roots. Iran's leaders learned well the lessons of the 1979 Revolution, when – operating from exile or in secret – they successfully used underground media, coupled with access to international media outlets, to communicate with revolutionaries, promote their cause and ultimately overthrow the Shah.[2] In turn, having appreciated the mobilizing power of the media, Iran's leadership has sought to manipulate and constrain the flow of information that is available to the Iranian people since seizing control of the country nearly forty years ago.

The resulting media environment within the Islamic Republic is profoundly circumscribed. Unauthorized media outlets are not tolerated, while authorized ones operate only as long as they do not challenge the political status quo, violate Islamic principles or the country's evolving legal code. Yet the interpretation of these rules and restrictions is highly inconsistent, and reflects the arbitrary nature of Iran's moral guardians.

Internationally, meanwhile, the apparatus of Iranian state media is used to promote the legitimacy of the regime; to amplify the narratives of Ali Khamenei, Iran's Supreme Leader; to popularize the country's perspectives on the Islamic faith; to offer support to disenfranchised Shi'a communities worldwide, and; to legitimate the Iranian regime's ongoing quest for regional hegemony. Well-resourced and extensive, this approach represents another means by which Iran's radical regime works to "export" its revolution beyond its borders.

CONSTRAINED AT HOME

Having experienced the power of the media firsthand during the ferment of the 1979 Islamic Revolution that brought them to power, Iran's leaders have tightly controlled Iran's domestic media environment since. The Iranian media landscape is dominated by state-sponsored media outlets that propagate regime messages and quasi-independent media outlets that are supported by various factions within Iran's political elite. Political debate is only minimally present and, when it occurs, is often driven by partisan attacks against political opponents. Official media, meanwhile, frequently discredits opponents and opposition to the regime writ large. Media outlets that oppose the government or offer dissenting opinions are persecuted and often shuttered.

Television remains the country's predominant news source. According to Freedom House, over 80 percent of Iran's citizens receive their news from television.[3] Iran's state television enterprise, as well its official radio broadcaster, is the Islamic Republic of Iran Broadcasting (IRIB)[4] which holds a legislated monopoly on radio and television broadcasting within the country. It operates five nationwide channels, a news channel, some 30 provincial channels, several international channels, eight nationwide radio networks, several provincial stations and an external news service. IRIB is controlled by a supervisory board that monitors and helps direct content, and which in turn is controlled by Iran's theological governing elites. A clear majority of Iranians (some research indicates as much as much as 86 percent) list IRIB as their most important source of information on TV, followed by the banned *BBC Persian*.[5]

IRIB is omnipresent on the radio waves as well, airing over 12 radio channels domestically and 30 radio stations designed for foreign audiences. By doing so, it competes with international radio broadcasters such as *Radio BBC*, the U.S.-based *Radio Farda*, Dutch *Radio Zamaneh*, *Radio France Internationale*, the *Voice of Israel* and Germany's *Deutsche Welle*. Radio is a far less influential media source, however, since comparatively few Iranians (just 16 percent) identify it as one of their most important sources of information.[6]

Print media is even less consequential, representing a regular source of news and information for just 10 percent of the country.[7] Nevertheless, as many as three hundred newspapers exist in Iran. Approximately 140 are published daily, but only a handful are national outlets.[8] Most are conservative and supported by various political factions, and are often used to attack and discredit political opponents. Examples of this include *Kayhan*, which is controlled by Iran's Supreme Leader, as well as *Iran*, a conservative government publication, and *Javan*, which is associated with Iran's clerical army, the Islamic Revolutionary Guard Corps (IRGC).[9]

Newspaper circulation is difficult to gauge, as numbers are distorted by various factions for both political and economic reasons. Consequently, no reliable figures on circulation exist, either in the public or private domains. However, Iran's largest paper is believed to be *Jam-e-Jam*, a conservative daily that is part of the IRIB network and which was estimated, as of 2014, to be read by 7.5% of the country's total population.[10] Its popularity is explained by its business model of geographic decentralization; *Jam-e-Jam* prints regionally, allowing it greater access to markets outside of the capital.[11]

In addition to its stranglehold over media outlets, the Iranian regime also attempts to control access to news content. The official Iranian news service, the Islamic Republic News Agency (IRNA), is operated by the Ministry of Culture and Islamic Guidance (MCIG), a body that – among other things – regulates Iran's domestic media. In addition to IRNA, there are a number of semi-official news agencies which promote the agendas of various government agencies. They include the FARS News Agency (Judiciary and the IRGC); the Mehr news agency (Ministry of Culture and Islamic Guidance); the Iranian Student News Agency, which is partially state funded; and ILNA, the Iranian Labor News Agency, which reports the official news of Iran's labor unions. [12]

International news outlets do have a presence within the Islamic Republic – albeit a tightly controlled one. The Iranian Ministry of Culture and Islamic Guidance officially states that there are 155 international media outlets from 32 countries that have offices in the country.[13] However, the actual number of active foreign sources of information operating inside the Islamic Republic is unknown, and is believed to be much lower.

Whatever the actual number, these outlets conduct their business under heavy restrictions. According to media watchdogs, foreign media outlets within Iran must provide authorities with advance notice of the stories they wish to publish. Additionally, visas are regularly denied to correspondents of those critical of the regime, and Iran exercises pressure on local staff and their families to control the reporting of international media outlets.[14] Foreign journalists who have run afoul of authorities have been jailed, as was *Washington Post* correspondent Jason Rezaian, a dual Iranian-American national who was held by Iranian authorities for 544 days.[15]

Nevertheless, despite extensive restrictions on both domestic and foreign media, Iran boasts a vibrant underground media market. While satellite dishes have officially been illegal in Iran since 1994, Iranians access international broadcasts in large numbers. According to a 2010 survey by BBC Monitoring, about 40 percent of the population watches satellite channels broadcast from abroad. Twelve percent of those polled in the same survey claimed to get their news from foreign television broadcasts.[16]

In this milieu, *BBC Persian* is among the most popular outlets, commanding as many as eight million viewers regularly.[17] This popularity, however, has made it a target of Iranian government, with BBC Persian staff facing routine harassment and official pressure, as well as disinformation campaigns designed to diminish its credibility and appeal. This conduct has been so egregious at times that it has prompted the channel to appeal to international organizations to restrain the Iranian regime.[18]

Meanwhile, U.S. government-sponsored broadcasters, namely the *Voice of America*'s Persian News Network and *Radio Free Europe/ Radio Liberty*'s *Radio Farda* are considered to be popular and have seen increased popularity following the recent protests in Iran. However, specific numbers for viewer and listenership are difficult to come by, with promoters and detractors of these services offering varying accounts of their reach into the Iranian population.[19]

In an effort to counter the reach of outlets such as *BBC Persian*, the Iranian regime has launched a number of fake news sites designed to disseminate erroneous information and dilute the effectiveness of foreign broadcasting.[20] These sites, in turn, are amplified by Facebook and other social media platforms, which have been used to significant effect to reinforce pro-regime narratives and to discredit foreign media sources. All of this is coupled with an extensive – and pervasive – regime strategy to curtail, manage and limit access to the Internet among ordinary Iranians.

TEHRAN VERSUS THE WORLD-WIDE WEB

Iran today ranks as one of the most "wired" nations in the Middle East, with 36 million Iranians, or over 44% of the population, possessing access to the internet.[21] It also boasts one of the world's most vibrant blogospheres. A 2009 survey by Harvard University's Berkman Center for Internet & Society estimated there are as many as sixty thousand Persian-language blogs,[22] although that figure has since receded somewhat as a result of government censorship.[23] In turn, the Internet has proven a powerful tool for mobilizing and organizing political opposition within Iran.

Social media platforms were heavily used in coordinating the protests of the "Green Movement" in 2009, when millions of Iranians took to the streets to protests political irregularities and the lack of economic opportunity. In response, the Iranian regime migrated onto the Internet as well, and "utilized information and communication technologies extensively in its successful suppression of the protests."[24] Subsequently, propelled by fears of domestic unrest (as well as well-founded worries over the potential of political ferment similar to that afflicting its Arab neighbors as part of the "Arab Spring"), the Iranian regime expanded its investments in Internet regulation, censorship and repression.[25] The result is one of the world's strictest Internet censorship regimes, which blocks or manipulates access to the World-Wide Web for millions, and which relies heavily on squelching content rather than drowning it a sea of messaging.

In pursuit of this effort, Iran's government has:
- Established an official clerical regulatory body, known as the Supreme Council on Cyberspace (SCC). Operating since 2012 under the guidance of Iran's Supreme Leader, the SCC is designed "to provide a centralized focal point for policy making and regulation of Iran's virtual space, effectively removing such authority from the executive, legislative and judiciary branches of government."[26]
- Pressured Internet Service Providers (ISPs) within the Islamic Republic to close sites that the government claims violate laws governing Internet content. These orders are enforced

by the regime's dedicated Cyber Police, a unit created to monitor online content.[27]

- Passed onerous regulations on access points within the Islamic Republic, such as Internet cafes, which are forced to record the personal information of customers–including vital data such as names, national identification numbers, and phone numbers–as well the installation of closed-circuit cameras to keep video logs of all customers accessing the World-Wide Web.[28]

- Expanded its control over social media platforms within the Islamic Republic, pursuant to a 2016 regulation from the Supreme Council of Cyberspace that requires foreign messaging companies to host Iranian user data on servers located in Iran.[29] This has allowed Iranian government officials to monitor and archive content accessed by ordinary Iranians.

- Collaborated with foreign technology firms, most conspicuously China's ZTE corporation, to expand monitoring of domestic phone, mobile and Internet communications.[30]

- Engaged in a wide-ranging campaign of intimidation and pressure against individuals seen by authorities as gatekeepers of the Internet. In August of 2016, the IRGC reported that it had questioned, detained, or issued warnings to more than 450 administrators of groups on various social media platforms regarding their hosting or promulgation of allegedly immoral content in an effort to promote censorship and limit debate.[31]

- Most recently, imposed a ban on popular social messaging app Telegram following the outbreak of renewed grassroots protests in late 2017, citing the platform's role in spreading social discontent.[32]

Most dramatic, however, has been Iran's efforts to establish its own version of the World-Wide Web – a "halal" or "second" internet that is designed to shunt online users to regime-approved resources and divert Iranians from accessing undesirable content. In 2016, the Iranian regime announced that it had completed the first phase of this national information network (NIN).[33] With a price tag of over $6 billion, the NIN is the costliest national telecommunications project in the history of the Islamic Republic, and showcases the regime's efforts to substantially cut reliance on, and access to, the broader Internet on the part of its citizens.[34]

Despite these efforts, the Internet remains a viable – if vulnerable – medium for free expression within the Islamic Republic. Iranians continue to access the Internet using a variety of anonymizing tools including virtual private networks (VPNs), rerouting programs such as TOR and other anonymizing software to enable communication. A 2016 survey conducted by the Iranian Students Polling Agency (ISPA), published by the *Financial Tribune*, showcased that – despite widespread regime bans on the same – some 53 percent of Iranians actively utilize social media networks, with the most popular among them being Telegram.[35] Social media, moreover, is used widely by more highly-educated, urban Iranians, with its rate of usage dropping dramatically (to just 42 percent of respondents) in rural areas.[36] Likewise, a variety of websites offer news, analysis, and commentary – although many have been banned or blocked in recent years for publishing reports seen as opposing the regime. Opposition sites, on the other hand, are restricted; these outlets need to be proactively sought out by users, and the penalties for accessing them can be significant.

Yet, even as its restricts Internet use at home, the Islamic Republic has been successful in using social media to its advantage globally. Much like Russia's "trolling" campaigns, the Iranian regime has convinced even its critics to repeat its narratives, particularly under the guise of rapprochement with the west. According to Mariam Memarsadeghi, a founder of Tavaana, an online training portal for Iranian civil society activists:

The Islamic Republic's control of the Internet goes well beyond censorship and surveillance. The regime makes nefarious use of social media to whitewash its rights abuses, galvanize support for its so-called moderates and manipulate international public opinion toward its key interests... All disinformation and propaganda strategies -- many via front groups, trolls and bots -- work to ensure regime survival, not ideological coherence. There is great pliability, in fact, when it comes to messaging, so much so that many Green Movement activists who fled Iran in 2009 and were granted political asylum in the U.S. became strong proponents of regime talking points regarding the nuclear program, America and Israel and even supported the regime's backing of Bashar Assad.[37]

LEGISLATING REPRESSION

Publicly, Iran declares that its citizens have both freedom of speech and opinion. Yet this rhetoric is refuted by the country's legal framework. In truth, Iranian media outlets are controlled by a well-established bureaucracy and legal system that are used to restrict the right of free speech and inhibit media freedom.

The Iranian Constitution establishes that the role of "the mass media (radio-television)... in pursuit of the evolutionary course of the Islamic Revolution, must be in the service of propagating Islamic culture. To this end it must try to benefit from healthy encounter of various thoughts and views. However, it must seriously refrain from propagating destructive and anti-Islamic attitudes."[38] This dictum drives the regime's media policy and has been used to control narratives surrounding sensitive political topics (such as the 2015 nuclear deal between Iran and the P5+1 powers known as the Joint Comprehensive Plan of Action).

But even more restrictive and potentially damaging is Article 24 of the Iranian constitution, which places the media at the mercy of an interpretation of morality carried out by the country's religious hierarchy. This has allowed Iranian clergy, and particularly its Supreme Leader, to control the media environment through interpretations of Islamic values that have enabled arbitrary prosecutions and helped keep the media off-balance. The effect is chilling; unsure of where the red lines of reporting and opinion lie, most mainstream journalists stay far clear of any coverage that could be construed as confronting Iran's ruling elite.

Regime constraints on the media are not simply outlined in the constitution, however. Iran has an established regulatory and judicial structure – codified in the country's Press Law – intended to silence independent journalists and control the country's domestic media environment.[39] The language of the law itself is vague and contradictory, allowing for arbitrary interpretation – a feature that has been used extensively to persecute journalists.[40]

Iran's press law is supported by the country's penal code, which includes multiple articles (Articles 262, 263, 286, 500, 513 and 514) designed to limit free expression, protect the narrative of the state as well as the reputation of its religious leaders. These articles outlaw "propaganda" against the state and "insults" to Islam – terms that are arbitrarily defined by Iran's leadership, but nonetheless carry heavy penalties for violators. More recent laws, passed in 2016, have expanded the immunity from criticism that is generally enjoyed by Iranian government officials.[41]

Bloggers, citizen journalists and online activists in Iran face the same restrictions as their colleagues in more traditional modes of media. A new body of laws enacted in 2009 establishes penalties for ill-defined online activity, such as libel, and for publishing materials deemed to damage "public morality" or promote the "dissemination of lies."[42] These regulations also extend the burden of censorship to the commercial market – in particular, Internet Service Providers, which are required to block the sites identified as carrying forbidden content by a committee headed by Iran's prosecutor general.[43]

In addition to the country's repressive legal framework, Iranian media is controlled by an established government bureaucracy. The main body enforcing press censorship is the Ministry of Culture and Islamic Guidance. Yet more important, although less frequently seen, is the control exerted by Iran's theological, military and governing elites, who in fact direct the activities of the Ministry and the persecution of opponents they deem to be of concern. The Ministry is authorized to arbitrarily close media outlets in an administrative process that occurs outside of public oversight but is heavily influenced by the regime's ruling hierarchy.

Most media cases are referred to specially created press courts, which are managed by the judiciary and which can impose criminal penalties on journalists. Although Iranian law mandates that these courts have juries, those bodies are handpicked by the Ministry of Culture and Islamic Guidance, Judiciary and by local authorities, and have only advisory powers. Extrajudicial courts, such as revolutionary courts, are also used by the government to persecute the media.

In addition to the courts, the Islamic Republic uses administrative, economic and judicial pressures, including the revocation of press licenses, which are necessary for publication, to keep media elements in line.

IRAN'S INTERNATIONAL OUTREACH

If Iran's domestic media strategy is based on repression, its international media strategy is more expansive, focused on creating core partnerships and broadcasting opportunities. Iran has a well-developed approach to engaging supportive populations, confronting enemies and building support for its narratives – particularly those that highlight Iran as the protector of disenfranchised populations and promote its hegemonic interests. In contrast to the extensive attention given today to

Russia's propaganda and disinformation campaigns, however, the external influence operations carried out by the Iranian regime are still poorly understood.

The Islamic Republic has become adept at using traditional state and international media to promote its interests – among them delegitimizing the West, projecting a credible image of its rule, and attracting defenders living beyond its borders. All of these narratives are designed to ensure regime expansion and survival, and they are promulgated via flexible, evolving messaging that often exerts influence in areas that have little to do with Shi'ism, such as in Afghanistan, or even with Islam altogether (like Venezuela). Iran's Supreme Leader himself has acknowledged that the Islamic Republic's international media strategies designed to emulate those of its allies, particularly Russia.[44]

These activities, however, remain poorly chronicled and even less well understood. There is a lack of information in the Arabic language regarding the Islamic Republic's influence and activities in the Middle East, and its consequent power to sway public opinion on the Arab "street" or with Iranians themselves. Similarly, in English, there has been only limited scrutiny of Iran's cyber-activities, or its manipulation of social media platforms denied to the Iranian people but which dominate discourse about Iranian interests.[45]

This constitutes a critical oversight. The Islamic Republic's financial, military and technological entities may represent the regime's hard power. Yet its soft power capabilities are just as potent – if not more so – in maintaining the appeal of the Islamic Republic's revolutionary brand.[46] As Michael Rubin of the American Enterprise Institute notes:

There's absolutely a media strategy in Iran. While U.S. officials embrace truth as the center of strategy on the philosophy that truthfulness builds credibility, the Iranian strategy is to throw stuff at the wall and see what sticks. It's an effective strategy against us. Determining the truth can sometimes take days or weeks and by then, the news cycle often moves on. But the Iranians can not only write the first draft of history but can also take advantage of any American mistakes which affirm their propaganda. The Iranians talk, for example, about how Americans in Afghanistan were seeking to corner the drug market. One American soldier then gets caught with opium? Suddenly, the Iranians will say, 'See, we were right all along.' Another way to think about it is that if winning hearts and minds has become central to U.S. military strategy, the Iranian military strategy is about turning hearts and minds against the Americans.[47]

Iran has invested considerable time and resources in order to erect the infrastructure necessary to implement this approach.[48] The most critical actor in this effort is the Islamic Radio and Television Union (IRTVU), which is part of the regime's Ministry of Culture and Islamic Guidance. Created in 2007, it provides member organizations with technical support in the service of Iran's international media strategy. IRTVU currently manages more than 200 radio and TV stations, the most powerful among them being the regime's Islamic Republic of Iran Broadcasting (IRIB) arm.

IRTVU is closely managed by the hierarchy of the Iranian regime. In 2015, at the IRTVU's annual conference, no less senior a figure than Iran's Supreme Leader, Ali Khamenei, extolled the importance of its activities. "Today," Khamenei said, "(the global) arrogance has created a great media empire. They distort and cover up news and they tell lies. This way, they promote their policies... We should do something in the face of this dangerous empire and this large media mafia that is in the hands of American and Zionist capitalists and cartels."[49]

IRIB operates several foreign language satellite channels, including the English-language *Press TV*, the Arabic *Al-Alam*, and *HispanTV*, a Spanish language station. HispanTV was formed in 2011 to reinforce ties between Iran and the "Bolivarian," revolutionary leftist states of Latin America, as well as to counter Western media dominance in the region.[50] Iran's international allies also assist in promulgating its narratives, including such media heavyweights as *Russia Today*'s Arabic language station and Qatar's flagship *Al Jazeera* channel, both of which sporadically promote Iranian narratives in support of their own foreign policy goals and to curry favor with Tehran. In fact, many see their support as more effective than the messaging of Iran's own state sponsored media and its surrogates.

Iran's international media strategy directly supports its hegemonic goals, particularly furthering the so-called "Axis of Resistance" strategy adopted by Iran, together with Syria, Lebanon's Hezbollah militia and the Palestinian terrorist movement Hamas, in 2010 as a means of confronting U.S. global influence. (Many consider Russia to be a supporter of the "axis" as well, so long as its actions support Russia's own foreign policy goals.[51]) In turn, Iran's media strategy is amplified by the broadcast organs of fellow "axis" members, among them Hezbollah's *Al-Manar* station and Lebanon's pan-Arab *Al-Mayadeen* channel. These outlets promulgate Iranian propaganda globally and provide technical support to other Arabic language television outlets as part of Iran's broader regional strategies. Media proxies supported by these efforts include *Al-Masirah* in Lebanon, as well as the *Al-Sahat* channel affiliated with Yemen's Houthi rebels and Libya's *Al-Nabaa*, both of which broadcast anti-Saudi programs as part of the Iranian regime's efforts to challenge Saudi Arabia's regional leadership.

To illustrate the importance placed on these regional allies, in October 2017, Ali Askari, director of the Islamic Republic of Iran Broadcasting (IRIB), travelled to Lebanon to visit Al Manar and Al Mayadeen and pledged greater support to these networks.[52] In addition, Askari met with Hassan Nasrallah, the Secretary-General of Hezbollah, to congratulate him for recent military successes. Nasrallah used the occasion to note the importance of the role that media outlets have played in these victories.[53]

Iraq represents a key theater for Iran's international media efforts. Since the Islamic Revolution in 1979, Iran's clerical regime has consistently attempted to influence the political tenor and trajectory of its western neighbor. The contemporary tools by which it seeks to do so include not only Iraq's assorted Shi'a militias (known locally as the Popular Mobilization Units, or PMUs), but also soft power tactics such as the proliferation of multiple radio and satellite television stations on Iraqi soil which are affiliated with assorted Iranian proxies. Many are focused on local issues, and are directly run by operatives of the IRGC's paramilitary arm, known as the Quds Force, with technical and staffing support provided by Hezbollah's networks.[54] Iran's media strategy in Iraq is based on diversification and grassroots media. Prior to the U.S. liberation of Iraq in 2003, Iranian media surrogates had already established a grassroots narrative aimed at portraying America as an invading army.[55] More recently Iran has used the conflict with the Islamic State terrorist group to support its narrative of protecting local populations, even as it continues to vilify U.S. involvement in internal Iraqi issues.[56]

Iran has deftly used its soft power in other regional arenas as well. Thus, in Bahrain, Tehran relies on news outlets that promote news which Bahraini media is not allowed to report on as a way of supplying Bahrain's marginalized Shi'a community with consistent narratives that support Iran's goals.[57] And in the Palestinian Territories, Iran provides technical and financial support to a range of television and radio stations as part of its efforts to promote Palestinian rejectionism and opposition to Israeli "occupation."[58]

These surrogate Arabic media outlets "are effective within certain sympathetic communities, such as disenfranchised Shia, who know who supports these outlets and what they stand for," notes Ambassador Alberto Fernandez, the President of the U.S. government's Middle East Broadcasting Networks. However, Fernandez notes, "other media Arabic media outlets such as *Al Jazeera* and *RT Arabic* that promote broader agendas which are supportive of their Iranian allies are far more effective" in swaying local populations to Tehran's cause.[59]

REPRESSION AT HOME, INFLUENCE ABROAD

As the foregoing suggests, Iran has succeeded in developing a sophisticated and heavy-handed media strategy. Domestically, it represses dissent and public opposition, while beyond its borders it executes an extensive disinformation and propaganda campaign that is designed to both confront its enemies and advance its narratives. Expectations of the advent of a more relaxed media environment within the Islamic Republic with the ascent to power of "moderates" like current Iranian President Hassan Rouhani have gone unfulfilled, and will likely remain unattainable. Nevertheless, domestic political opposition continues to operate in spite of the regime's extensive attempts at media control.

This, in turn, affords a window of opportunity for the international community. Fast moving technological innovation inherently favors Iran's opposition. Over time, the Iranian regime will find it more and more difficult to control the country's internal narrative, as Iranians acquire increasingly sophisticated tools to subvert government censorship. Iran's highly educated youth population craves unbiased information and increased access to international news. Support from the international community therefore is critical to expanding unfiltered media access for Iran's citizens in the face of increasingly onerous government strictures.

At the same time, the international community must begin to understand and seriously counter Iran's international media strategy. So far, Iran's international communications have been effective in diluting Western narratives, delegitimizing Western allies and enlisting sympathetic populations to the regime's cause. This broad-based strategy remains unchecked and unaddressed by the United States and its international partners.

It should not be. Today, the U.S. has an opportunity to establish a media strategy that helps isolate the Iranian regime, discredit it domestically, and marginalize its influence among foreign populations. So far, however, Western nations have not formulated a serious plan to challenge Iranian efforts to win over disenfranchised populations and recruit new allies.

ENDNOTES

1. Freedom House, "Freedom of the Press 2017," 2017, https://free-domhouse.org/report/freedom-press/2017/iran; Reporters Without Borders, 2018 World Press Freedom Index, 2018, https://rsf.org/en/ranking.
2. Anabelle Sreberny-Mohammadi and Ali Mohammadi, *Small media, Big Revolution* (University of Minnesota Press, 1994).
3. Freedom house, "Freedom of the Press 2015," 2015, https://free-domhouse.org/report/freedom-press/2015/iran.
4. Ibid.
5. Alberto Zanconato, "Iran-Media Landscape," European Journalism Center, 2018, https://medialandscapes.org/country/iran/television.
6. BBC," Iran country profile – Media in numbers," June 11, 2013, http://www.bbc.com/news/world-middle-east-22863937.
7. Ibid.
8. Greg Bruno, "The Media Landscape in Iran," Council on Foreign Relations, July 22, 2009, https://www.cfr.org/backgrounder/media-landscape-iran.
9. Shahram Rafizadeh and Mahsa Alimardani, "The Political Affiliations of Iranian Newspapers," Iran Media Program, University of Pennsylvania, 2013, https://repository.upenn.edu/cgi/viewcontent.cgi?article=1008&context=iranmediaprogram.
10. Arash Karami, "Tehran Poll: 60% Believe Media has Little or No Freedom," *Al-Monitor*, September 22, 2014, https://www.al-monitor.com/pulse/originals/2014/05/tehran-citizens-believe-media-not-free.html.
11. Zanconato, "Iran-Media Landscape."
12. Ibid.
13. Ministry of Culture and Islamic Guidance, "List of Foreign Media Offices," n.d., https://foreignmedia.farhang.gov.ir/fa/pressoffices
14. Mana Neyestani, "How Iran tries to control news coverage by foreign-based journalists," RSF, September 6, 2017, https://rsf.org/en/news/how-iran-tries-control-news-coverage-foreign-based-journalists/.
15. Freedom House, "Freedom of the Press 2017."
16. BBC, "Iran country profile – Media in numbers."
17. Magdalena Wojcieszak, Briar Smith and Mahmood Enayat, "Finding a way: How Iranians reach for news and information," Iran Media

Project, University of Pennsylvania, 2012, http://www.global.asc.
upenn.edu/fileLibrary/PDFs/FindingaWay.pdf; See also Bruno,
"The Media Landscape In Iran."

18. See, for example, Kasra Naji, "BBC UN Appeal: Stop Iran Harass-
ing Persian Service Staff," *BBC Persian*, March 12, 2018, http://
www.bbc.com/news/world-middle-east-43334401.

19. The Broadcasting Board of Governors, the U.S. government body
that oversees all official U.S. international media, claims that nearly one in four adult Iranians (23.4 percent) watch the Persian News
Network or listen to Farda broadcasts. See Broadcasting Board of
Governors, "Priority Profile: Iran," n.d. However, critics of U.S.
broadcasting toward Iran have argued that the actual market share
captured by American programming is significantly more modest.

20. Thomas Fox-Brewster, "Inside The 7-Year-Old Iranian Propaganda
Machine Producing Fake BBC News," *Forbes*, February 28, 2018,
https://www.forbes.com/sites/thomasbrewster/2018/02/28/
bbc-iran-fake-news/#39223d2f54f1.

21. "Iran," Central Intelligence Agency *World Factbook*, n.d., https://
www.cia.gov/library/publications/the-world-factbook/geos/ir.ht-
ml.

22. John Kelly and Bruce Etling, "Mapping Iran's Online Public: Politics and Culture in the Persian Blogosphere," Berkman Center,
Harvard University, April 2008, https://cyber.harvard.edu/sites/
cyber.law.harvard.edu/files/Kelly&Etling_Mapping_Irans_On-
line_Public_2008.pdf.

23. Ibid.

24. Ilan Berman, "Iranian Devolution: Tehran Fights the Digital Future," *World Affairs Journal*, Fall 2015, http://www.worldaffairs-
journal.org/article/iranian-devolution-tehran-fights-digital-future.

25. Ibid.

26. "Iran," in *Freedom on the Net 2012* (Freedom House, 2012),
https://freedomhouse.org/report/freedom-net/2012/iran.

27. Media Landscapes, *Iran Digital Media Report*, n.d., https://medi-
alandscapes.org/country/iran/media/digital-media.

28. See, for example, Golnaz Esfandiari, "Iran Announces New Restrictions for Internet Cafes," *Radio Free Europe/Radio Liberty*, January
4, 2012, https://www.rferl.org/a/iran_announces_new_internet_
restrictions/24442396.html.

29. "Iran Orders Social Media Sites to Store Data Inside Country,"
Reuters, May 29, 2016, https://www.reuters.com/article/inter-

net-iran/iran-orders-social-media-sites-to-store-data-inside-country-idUSL8N18Q0IN.
30. Steve Stecklow, "Special Report: Chinese firm helps Iran spy on citizens," Reuters, March 22, 2012, http://www.reuters.com/article/2012/03/22/us-iran-telecoms-idUSBRE82L0B820120322.
31. Freedom House, "Freedom of the Press 2017."
32. See, for example, Dani Deahi, "Iran has Banned Telegram after Claiming the App Encourages 'Armed Uprisings,'" *The Verge*, May 1, 2018, https://www.theverge.com/2018/5/1/17306792/telegram-banned-iran-encrypted-messaging-app-russia.
33. BBC, "Iran Media Profile."
34. Internet Monitor, "Iran's National Information Network: faster Speeds, but at what cost."
35. "53% of Iranians Use Social Media," *Financial Tribune*, January 9, 2016, https://financialtribune.com/articles/economy-sci-tech/33702/53-of-iranians-use-social-media.
36. Ibid.
37. Mariam Memarsadeghi, interview with the author, April 2018.
38. *Constitution of the Islamic Republic of Iran*, October 24, 1979, http://www.servat.unibe.ch/icl/ir00000_.html.
39. World Intellectual Property Organizations, "Iran Press Law," n.d., http://www.wipo.int/wipolex/en/details.jsp?id=11389.
40. Press Law, March 19, 1986, http://www.parstimes.com/law/press_law.html.
41. Freedom House, "Freedom of the Press 2017."
42. Open Net Initiative, "Internet Filtering in Iran," 2009, https://opennet.net/sites/opennet.net/files/ONI_Iran_2009.pdf.
43. *Computer Crimes Act*, June 18, 2009, https://www.unodc.org/res/cld/document/computer-crimes-act_html/Computer_Crimes_Act.pdf.
44. Memarsadeghi, Interview with the author.
45. Ibid
46. Ibidem.
47. Michael Rubin, interview with author, April 2018.
48. Michael Rubin, "Strategies Underlying Iranian Soft Power," Foreign Military Studies Office, March 7, 2017, http://www.aei.org/publication/strategies-underlying-iranian-soft-power/.
49. Office of the Supreme Leader, "Ayatollah Khamenei receives the Participants in the 8th Summit of the General Assembly of the Islamic Radio and Television Union (IRTVU) and the 6th General Assembly

of the Ahlul Bayt World Assembly," August 17, 2015, http://www. leader.ir/en/media/13484/Ayatollah-Khamenei-receives-the-participants-in-the-8th-summit-of-the-General-Assembly-of-the-Islamic-Radio-and-Television-Union-(IRTVU)-and-the-6th-General-Assembly-of-the-Ahlul-Bayt-World-Assembly; "Iran urges Islamic media to defy U.S. influence in region," China.org.cn, August 17, 2015, http://www.china.org.cn/world/Off_the_Wire/2015-08/17/content_36321684.htm.

50. For a detailed discussion, see Joseph M. Humire and Ilan Berman, eds., *Iran's Strategic Penetration of Latin America* (Lanham: Lexington Books, 2014).

51. Lamont Colucci, "Beware Iran's Axis of Resistance," *U.S. News and World Report*, February 23, 2018, https://www.usnews.com/opinion/world-report/articles/2018-02-23/irans-axis-of-resistance-is-a-direct-threat-to-the-us.

52. "Aoun Welcomes Director of Iran's Radio and Television," National News Agency (Beirut), October 18, 2017, http://nna-leb.gov.lb/en/show-news/84446/nna-leb.gov.lb/en.

53. Colucci, "Beware Iran's Axis of Resistance."

54. Michael Knights, "The Role of Broadcast Media in Influence Operations in Iraq," Washington Institute for Near East Policy *Policy-Watch* 758, May 19, 2003, http://www.washingtoninstitute.org/policy-analysis/view/the-role-of-broadcast-media-in-influence-operations-in-iraq.

55. Rubin, "Strategies Underlying Iranian Soft Power."

56. Ibid.

57. Ibidem.

58. See, for example, Islamic Radios and Televisions Union, "Six Palestinian Media Institutions have Delivered the Islamic Radios and Televisions Union Certificate of Membership, n.d., http://irtvu.com/article.php?id=375841.

59. Amb. Alberto Fernandez, interview with author, April 2018.

THE NEW DIGITAL GUERILLAS: ISIS AND AFTER
Haroon K. Ullah

As the terrorist group known as the Islamic State, or ISIS, loses ever more ground on the physical battlefield, it faces a challenge in another arena as well: the battlefield of ideas. The call for followers to travel to the "caliphate" in support of ISIS, which propelled an estimated 40,000 foreign fighters into its ranks between 2014 and 2017,[1] has been markedly reduced, if not rendered altogether obsolete. This has forced ISIS to alter and accelerate its messaging tactics, to enter the digital realm, and to harbor in a virtual safe haven. The group's messengers now tell supporters to remain where they are and wage war for ISIS wherever they live. Their brand is shifting from that of an ideological organization seeking territory to an umbrella brand for grievances, psychopathy and hatred. Instead of recruiting in order to gain terrain and erect a "righteous" state, ISIS is now increasingly promoting a clandestine, decentralized, international insurgency for marginalized and impressionable youth.

Meanwhile, the foreign terrorist fighters who once made their way to the Middle East are now heading in the other direction, seeking to escape the battlefield and return to their home countries, from where they can develop local networks and launch attacks. As a consequence, the target audience of ISIS extremism is no longer the group, but the individual "soldier." The organization's safe haven on the dark web and encrypted social media platforms has limited its reach, but the resulting call is now more personalized, and thus more persuasive and easier to heed. Halting its ability to leverage these private spaces has become crucial to defeating ISIS.

Yet the challenges posed by digital anonymity and hidden association make it harder to identify and track the inspired, self-radicalized attacker, as we discovered in bloody retrospect in Dhaka, Medina, Kabul, Ansbach and elsewhere. Keeping abreast of the activity in the digital underworld has become critical to the safety of citizens in the U.S. and nations around the world. Countering the anonymous use of the Internet by violent extremists has consequently become a core focus in the fight to defeat ISIS and its ideological fellow travelers.

BLURRING LINES

Over the past decade, advances in digital technology have contributed to seismic rebellions across the Muslim World. They have underpinned uprisings led by Islamists, and have harnessed social media and associated networking technologies to harass and defeat secular and/or corrupt regimes. These same tools have also given digital rebels the capacity to wage guerrilla warfare on their own terms and without the need for massive budgets – in the process, enabling the weaponization of information. From recruitment, mobilization and organization to fundraising, censorship evasion, image protection and the formation of unlikely alliances between governments and private-sector conglomerates, the ability to exploit social media has been a game-changer in Muslim-majority countries.

It should come as no surprise, then, that leaders and officials in those countries display a conspicuous distrust of the Internet. Muslim governments routinely claim that social media "causes unrest." Turkey's ruler, Recep Tayyip Erdogan, has gone so far as to call Twitter "a menace."[2] And he's right. If enough citizens are unhappy, Twitter and other social media technologies present a significant threat to power. Even in heavily censored countries, the Big Brother dynamic has been inverted; these days, Little Brother does the watching, and leaders are left to worry.

The numbers tell the story. As of this writing, more than 125 million of the 381 million people living in the Middle East and North Africa (MENA) have access to the Internet.[3] This cohort is also overwhelmingly young; about 60 percent of the overall MENA population is less than 30 years old, and more than 53 million people are actively engaged with social media and recognize its power to hound the establishment.[4] As clearly demonstrated by the peer-to-peer organization of the Arab Spring revolts that raged from 2010 to 2012, young citizens empowered by digital connections could challenge the old guard and, in many Muslim countries, push them to the brink.[5] As one message on social networks during the 2011 Egypt revolution put it: "If your government shuts down your Internet, it's time to shut down your government."[6]

Governments fought back with a combination of digital and brute physical force, but the fight for hearts, minds and power continues to rage across the virtual battlefield. Of course, political forces have long taken advantage of new communications technologies to spread propaganda and incite fear. The wars of the 19th century demonstrated the earliest practical usage of telegrams for relaying commands and coordinating movement between battalions in real-time. In World War II, the use of radio allowed effective coordination between air and land forces, but also delivered messages designed to inspire allied citizens or sow fear and panic in enemy countries. Today, the overall sophistication of the means has improved dramatically, but the ends remain essentially the same.

ISIS and other extremist groups employ the same tactics through increasingly powerful digital channels. They use the dark web to plan and execute devastating attacks in Paris, Brussels, Hanover, Dhaka and Orlando, and then magnify the psychological power of the assaults through social media channels. ISIS has become "the first terrorist group to hold both physical and digital territory," in the words of Jared Cohen, the CEO of Jigsaw and an adjunct senior fellow at the Council on Foreign Relations.[7] On the ground, its troops murder, pillage and oppress. On the Web, its "digital warriors" post gory content intended to glorify the organization as an unassailable and righteous caliphate, sending warnings of what lies in store for those who choose to oppose them.

In fact, the recent conflicts in the Middle East offer a stark reminder of how the lines between physical and digital warfare have blurred. Extremist groups have spread fear and panic across the globe. They have created or hijacked hashtags for use as digital weapons, exaggerating news of small-scale ambushes or highlighting heinous crimes against helpless individuals as massive victories on the battlefield. But their primary source of strength does not reside in the strategic prowess of their leaders or the barbarism of their soldiers. Rather, it manifests in their ability to harness the power of social media and use it to strengthen their control on both physical and digital terrain. Put another way, social media has helped to transform a ragtag militia with substandard weapons and an uncanny taste for violence into a global force that threatens the combined military might of some of the most sophisticated armies in the modern world. ISIS and its army of digital warriors have successfully used Twitter, Facebook and Instagram both to establish control locally and to spread disinformation and fear globally.

Driving Forces

The online recruitment and engagement strategy employed by extremists mimics the digital presence fostered by a multinational firm's public relations department. Blogs, comments, videos and pictures posted on social media and other online forums are produced with professional precision and choreography to increase their appeal and authenticity, especially for young audiences. ISIS has recruited professional cameramen, choreographers and marketing experts, who spend a considerable amount of effort and time to ensure that the organization's images, videos and messages contain all the necessary ingredients for engaging, compelling and authentic content. The organization supplements its professionally crafted content with the large number of personal accounts created by ISIS-affiliated fighters, who regularly post pictures and videos of their daily lives, further increasing authenticity and appeal by humanizing themselves as people with similar interests and characteristics. Potential ISIS sympathizers on Internet forums and social media are promptly identified, targeted and recruited using a subtle strategy that can take months and years to work, but which lands new converts at a higher rate than one might imagine.

While no one can point to a single, uniform path to radicalization, we can identify several common factors that guide most extremists like ISIS. The Islamic State and other terrorist organizations regularly exploit grievances by offering young recruits a sense of purpose, belonging or adventure. They rally new proponents around a powerful ideology, usually one that plays off of religious obligations. And they rely on charismatic influencers who often might fail in most recruitment efforts, but who know how to identify the best targets and which messages and channels to use to optimize their chances with them.

Grievances

ISIS and other groups seek to exploit political grievances against governments by citing their policies in the region and by highlighting alienation and discrimination against Muslim communities around the world. In Muslim-majority countries, extremist organizations will stoke the perception that governments repress religious freedoms, violate human rights, restrict political expression and do little to build economic opportunity. In the Arab world, a strong sectarian dimension pervades the ISIS narrative, as the group regularly calls on Muslims to defend Sunni communities against the Shi'a. And in many other parts of the world, the presence of "push factors" such as poverty, illiteracy and poor education provide fertile soil in which extremism can grow. ISIS and other groups also try to exploit a variety of psychological factors, including issues of identity and spiritual imperfection. Some recruits seek to make up for past indiscretions and engage in "self-cleansing" by embracing the terrorists' vision of Islam. Although the Islamic State's use of violence is rejected by Muslims generally, their grievance narrative resonates broadly.

Ideology

Terrorists use a warped version of Islam to argue that individuals may use terrorism to defend their communities around the world. As a part of this narrative, they misuse and exploit the concepts to call for the reestablishment of the Caliphate. ISIS has added an additional element to this message; the group manipulates the historically grounded respect many Muslims hold for the early Islamic caliphs, claiming that its small band of fighters, through divine support, will capture territories, fulfill the vision of a truly religious state and defend the *ummah* (the Islamic community as a whole). Terrorist groups use these concepts to instill a sense of purpose, empowerment, adventure and religious obligation and reward.

The role of ideology is particularly important because it accentuates all of the other factors in the radicalization process. If an individual has a grievance in his or her personal life, extremist recruiters will aim to sway them with twisted ideological ideals that provide a sense of purpose and reward. If the grievance is political in nature, the terrorists tweak their message to emphasize a vision of an authority that empowers them and their allies. Thus, ideology becomes the vehicle, justification or excuse that violent extremists use to act on their grievances.

Influencers

Recruits rarely radicalize on their own. In most cases, a figure in their community or an individual or group acting online seduces them with a powerful blend of grievance and ideology. Research shows that young recruits typically come from middle-class families in urban areas. The geographical concentration of this smaller middle-class cohort helps explain why Islamist parties tend to do better in provincial, regional and local elections than at the national level. In fact, studies show that most recruits join terrorist groups because of identity grievances, not poverty or related environmental factors. Most of these recruits have studied at public universities and are fed up with the corruption and mayhem around them. Extremist groups offer an effective change narrative–a black-and-white answer for how to alter society by applying a different set of rules. In the absence of other solutions, the clear-cut answers provided by religious extremists look especially enticing.

Coherent vision

Contrary to conventional wisdom, extremists like ISIS are not selling a dark, medieval narrative. In fact, an estimated eighty percent of extremist messaging can be categorized as positive messaging.[8] But extremists are good at customer segmentation, and simultaneously deliver a grotesque and dark message to English-speaking audiences and very different ones in Arabic, French and Russian (the top three languages in which ISIS messages). This is evident in the way ISIS markets itself as well. As the group's recruitment videos make plain, ISIS is selling a consumerist lifestyle, and a western-modeled, efficient governance structure free of corruption. This is no return to the Dark Ages and archaic traditions, in other words. It is, rather, the new caliphate on steroids, bigger and better than that of the Ottomans.

Support networks

Significant, too, is the role of religious leaders. The most popular person on Twitter in the Middle East is not an actor or politician, but an extremist Saudi cleric named Mohammed Al-Arefe. With more than 18 million followers and a prolific presence on Snap and other digital platforms, he is today one of the biggest reasons that young people from Saudi Arabia and elsewhere in the Middle East have mobilized to join ISIS and other Islamic extremists in Iraq and Syria. Religious leaders like Al-Arefe are an integral part of the ISIS "fanboy" network, and play an indispensable role in propagating the organization's messages and mobilizing the masses to its cause.

TURNING THE TIDE

The scope and sophistication of the media strategy currently employed by ISIS and other Islamic extremists requires Western governments to adapt their messaging in response. Simply messaging to mass audiences will sway no one. In order to ensure that positive counter-messaging is effective and impactful, Western outreach must be tailored to four key audiences: fence sitters, immediate influencers, cultural influencers and the general public.

When reaching out to fence-sitters, the tiny fraction of the world's 1.6 billion Muslims who seriously consider joining ISIS or other organizations, messengers who hold extreme ideological views but don't support extremist groups can have the greatest influence. Such messengers include ISIS defectors and members of groups that have condemned other extremist organizations. Videos of defectors in recent case studies have shown not only attitudinal shifts but also behavioral shifts, which is the holy grail of prevention programs.[9] Because ideological justifications push many fence-sitters to act, Western messaging should demonstrate the damage that ISIS and other groups are inflicting. It is also necessary to open new and attractive avenues for fence-sitters with messaging about positive alternative choices. Programs like "Redirect," pioneered by Jigsaw, Google's in-house think tank, off-ramp young individuals searching for more information about ISIS by placing seemingly innocuous ads to lead them down a different "customer journey."[10]

Authentic statements from friends and family members impacted by terrorist violence will resonate with fence-sitters and immediate influencers alike. By aligning our efforts with those of immediate influencers, the United States and its allies can amplify a positive message to susceptible young men and women. For example, one Pakistani program called *Ho Yaqeen* played on this idea of getting key influencers from arts/culture to reach out to vulnerable youth.[11] The campaign would later become so successful it was sponsored by Coca Cola and disseminated nationwide. As we widen the lens to integrate cultural influencers and general audiences, positive messaging will have greater influence when targeted at the very start of the "pre-hate journey," guiding young minds toward mutually beneficial pursuits from the start. Ideally, this messaging should come from non-governmental sources, but government messaging also can exert a positive influence with these target audiences, who are less likely to dismiss it as propaganda.

In addition to segmentation by level of radicalization, audiences should be segmented by geography. ISIS messages, for example, vary depending on the region they are targeting. In the Arab World, its narrative is largely sectarian, arguing that Sunni Muslims have an obligation to end Shi'a abuses and expansion in Iraq and Syria. In addressing European audiences, the Islamic State emphasizes the alienation and discrimination that is faced by some Muslim communities there. And in addressing American and Canadian audiences, ISIS challenges Muslims to leave their comfortable living conditions and to "fill the spiritual voids" in their lives by defending fellow Muslims suffering elsewhere. As a result, traditional counter messaging, entailing tit-for-tat narratives, tends to be effective in reinforcing previously held beliefs and affiliations. For example, accurate independent reporting on American Muslims (who serve in the U.S. military, as teachers, police, doctors etc.) has proven to be a useful antidote to ISIS propaganda.

Because of its online sophistication and current influence on the Middle East and globally, ISIS provides a good example of how the United States and its allies might segment audiences on today's information battlefield in order to effectively counter Islamist messaging. These include:

Hyperlocality – Messaging that resonates well in Jordan might fall flat in Egypt or Belgium. With limited resources, those fighting extremists in different countries or cities need to ensure that messaging and programs are tailored for those targeted audiences. Just as ISIS thinks about segmented audiences, so too will the United States and its partners need to produce different media in different national and regional vernacular. This organic approach can help to add authenticity and therefore carry more force among prospective viewers.

Monitoring – Effective media content requires time-intensive work with local partners to ensure proper storyboarding, tone and language. ISIS doesn't simply outsource things to contractors. Rather, it has a rabid fan base that is passionate about media, and much of the content the group produces goes through rigorous pre-testing, including focus groups. In turn, responses to ISIS messaging must adopt the same level of granularity and attention to detail in order to serve as potent antidotes.

Visual narratives – Music, dramas and animation are game-changers. ISIS, for example, has its own version of "Game of Thrones," as well as interactive online games and choose your own adventure fantasy software. But this same medium can be harnessed to dilute ISIS appeal as well. In 2016, for instance, the Saudi TV show *Selfie* was a top-rated program in the Middle East and directly took on ISIS through satire that took aim and poked fun at the group's caliphate. This success is instructive; the ability to visually tell dramatic stories and tragedies of terrorism resonates deeply with key audiences.

Partnership with key influencers – It is necessary to amplify credible voices and partner with locally rooted groups. Media partners who are well-respected and notable leaders in their field, whether documentaries, music, interfaith or animation, "move the needle" in terms of both viewership and credibility. These influences can deliver a positive message in a way that resonates with target audiences – and does so more authentically than foreign content alone ever could.

Audience awareness – In its messaging, ISIS and its ilk wield a formidable comparative advantage: deeply integrated into local communities, they can deploy communications and social welfare programs, immediately sense which efforts work best, and then adapt their plans based on that knowledge. By contrast, big governments or large corporations and organizations with less access and a bigger bureaucracy are not able to learn and adapt as quickly. Accordingly, serious effort must be given by the United States and its partners to gaining greater awareness of target audiences, and to countering the structural advantages in the "feedback loops" that violent extremist groups enjoy.

Multimedia linkage – As we have learned, the popularity of certain programming can elevate that of others. In the case of the Saudi program *Selfie*, producers successfully linked the TV and radio versions of the show, and found that the target audience followed both. Such an experience is instructive, and highlights the value of linkage in programming content and platforms – something that is a departure from the traditional view of standalone platforms designed for discrete goals. In turn, feedback mechanisms, such as SMS and social media platforms, can allow for additional interactive engagement with viewers.

A range of interventions – Among the most powerful lessons that can be drawn from observing extremist group behavior is the need for a range of inhibitor messaging to prevent individuals from moving down the path toward extremist violence. Deploying a range of media products helps to present multiple tipping points for changing behavior and channeling grievances toward more productive actions. This range of interventions allows for more balanced content to be presented to viewers when and where they are ready to receive it.

Broad focus – To attract audiences, anti-hate programming needs to inspire positive outcomes as well as discourage extremism. Presenting alternative narratives of young people who have succeeded in life against great odds attracts audiences and portrays viable alternatives to extremism. Thus, an Afghan program called *Khudi* focused on young people, like Pakistani activist (and Nobel Prize laureate) Malala Yousefzai, who overcame odds to become community builders. It became compelling content on both TV and digital sources.

Research – Research is necessary in order to determine which medium works best for which audience. For instance, rock music may resonate in Egypt, but it does not do so as well in Malaysia. Research provides these sorts of insights, guiding communicators regarding what kinds of programming to organize in which locations, and enabling groups on the ground to constantly retool content based on regular feedback.

Public-private partnerships – Fiscal realities dictate that local and international stakeholders will have to do more with less in coming years. Increasingly, efforts to combat hate will need to overlap with the interests and activities of NGOs and the private sector, in order to combine various efforts and unleash more volunteerism. A number of such private sector efforts already exist. Facebook, for example, has sponsored a program called Peer to Peer (P2P), which brings together over 200 universities worldwide and incentivizes students to compete on projects to counter extremism.[12] This program has organically spawned a community of young people who are driving change at the local level – effectively, harnessing a network to defeat a network in a method not so dissimilar from that advocated by military commanders.

In turn, the young activists of P2P and its analogues will explore new opportunities with local partners, develop innovative programming and build relationships with key influencers. In order to do so, however, they will need to be trained and equipped with the intellectual tools to effectively counter hate messaging. There are now many examples of such training courses, like the AVE (Against Violent Extremism) network initially seeded by Google.[13] Such networks provide a critical digital platform for young people to talk about peace, conflict resolution and other measures.

A startup model – To be sustainable, efforts to counter extremism should adopt a startup model, in which organizations gather international resources and use seed funding to help a project take shape and get it off the ground. Research shows that the most effective projects are not the two million dollar grants, but rather those that are smaller (ranging from $2,000 to $25,000). The reason is practical; most local NGOs simply cannot absorb large scale infusions of resources and utilize it effectively. Small seed money, on the other hand, can go a long way. Many local NGOs work in conflict-ridden areas, where refugees and internally-displaced persons, especially youth, are particularly vulnerable to recruitment into ISIS and affiliated extremist groups. Insurgent groups capitalize on this dynamic, recruiting heavily in these areas and camps. In turn, counter-hate programming needs to be implemented by relevant NGOs to support refugees and internally displaced persons as such situations arise.

GRAVE NEW WORLD

The Islamic State effectively broke the conventional mold of terrorism with its social-media savvy. When the group first emerged onto the scene, few noticed. Yet its corrosive message and appeal has resonated far beyond its territorial caliphate, which is now being eroded. ISIS' success in the digital realm, in turn, has inspired others. Groups like Tahrir al Sham, the Salafi-jihadist group that operates as al-Qaeda in Syria, are beginning to realize that winning the physical war is much less important than winning online. As a result, even as the United States and its partners grapple with countering ISIS messaging, they must also prepare for the rise of what could be called ISIS 3.0 – a future evolution of the Islamist model to even more adroitly exploit the digital domain for both messaging and attacks.

Today, there is a growing understanding among diplomats and policymakers of how radicalism spreads and gains traction within different communities. By identifying how ideas go viral, and how they can best be countered, we can more effectively compete on what is perhaps the most decisive battlefield of all in the fight against Islamic extremism: that of ideas.

ENDNOTES

1. Richard Barrett, *Beyond The Caliphate: Foreign Fighters and the Threat of Returnees* (The Soufan Center, October 2017), http://thesoufancenter.org/wp-content/uploads/2017/10/Beyond-the-Caliphate-Foreign-Fighters-and-the-Threat-of-Returnees-TSC-Report-October-2017-v2.pdf.
2. Divya Avasthy, "Turkey's Erdogan Blocks Access to Twitter Accusing Gülen of Social Media Attacks," *International Business Times*, March 21, 2014, https://www.ibtimes.co.uk/turkeys-erdogan-blocks-access-twitter-accusing-gulen-social-media-attacks-1441196.
3. Emma Murphy, "Youth Challenges in the MENA Region," *Middle East Monitor*, November 4, 2014, https://www.middleeastmonitor.com/20141104-youth-challenges-in-the-mena-region/.
4. Ibid.
5. Ibidem.
6. As cited in Christian Vachon, "Tonight in Cairo, the Parliament is Surrounded," *The Awl*, January 25, 2011, http://www.theawl.com/2011/01/tonight-in-cairo-the-parliament-is-surrounded
7. Jared Cohen, "Digital Counterinsurgency: How to Marginalize the Islamic State Online," *Foreign Affairs*, November/December 2015, https://www.foreignaffairs.com/articles/middle-east/digital-counterinsurgency.
8. See, for example, Haroon K. Ullah, *Digital World War: Islamists, Extremists, and the Fight for Cyber Supremacy* (New Haven: Yale University Press, 2017), 19, 38-39; See also Elizabeth Bodine-Baron et al., *Examining ISIS Support and Opposition Networks on Twitter* (Santa Monica: RAND, 2016), https://www.rand.org/content/dam/rand/pubs/research_reports/RR1300/RR1328/RAND_RR1328.pdf.
9. See, for example, Anne Speckhard and Ahmet Yayla, "How ISIS Defectors Can Help Us Beat Terror," *TIME*, August 1, 2016, http://time.com/4401066/isis-defectors-terror/; See also Allison McDowell-Smith, Anne Speckhard, and Ahmet S. Yayla, "Beating ISIS in the Digital Space: Focus Testing ISIS Defector Counter=Narrative Videos with American College Students," *Journal for Deradicalization* no. 10, 2017, http://journals.sfu.ca/jd/index.php/jd/article/view/83.
10. The Redirect Method, n.d., https://redirectmethod.org.
11. For more on *Ho Yaqeen*, see Zehra Nabi, "Highlighting Heroes:

The Ho Yaqeen Campaign," *NewsLine*, June 2012, http://newslinemagazine.com/magazine/highlighting-heroes-the-ho-yaqeen-campaign/.

12. EdVenture Partners, "Peer to Peer: Facebook Global Digital Challenge," n.d., https://edventurepartners.com/peer-to-peer-facebook-global-digital-challenge/.

13. Online at http://www.againstviolentextremism.org.

THE CHALLENGE FACING U.S. INTERNATIONAL MEDIA
Robert Bole

In 2010, two stunning events heralded a new chapter in how information, especially digital platforms, could be used to advance foreign policy interests. The first was the publication by information (and sometime propaganda) clearinghouse Wikileaks of the "Afghan War Diaries," a cache of over 75,000 U.S. government documents relating to America's prosecution of Operation Enduring Freedom. The second and subsequent disclosure, which came at the start of the political ferment of the "Arab Spring" in the Middle East and North Africa, was a massive dump of 400,000 documents relating to U.S. involvement in Iraq, and 251,000 assorted U.S. diplomatic documents and cables.

Together, these two events underscored the newfound power of small groups to harness information warfare to affect foreign affairs, and to undermine the stability and credibility of nation states. They effectively turn strategist Paul Nitze's infamous dictum, that "We'll make the policy and then you can put it on your damn radios,"[1] on its ear. Today, media is emerging as a preeminent tool to shape the ground upon which foreign policy is made.

The rise of revanchist, authoritarian powers that have mastered the new information environment in order to influence foreign audiences, to undermine the liberal democratic order and its institutions, and to roll back domestic freedoms offers the biggest test to date for U.S. International Media (USIM) – the five international media networks (the *Voice of America, Radio Free Europe/Radio Liberty*, the Middle East Broadcasting Network, *Radio Free Asia* and *Radio/TV Marti*) by which the U.S. exposes foreign publics to democratic ideals, and the billion dollar agency that oversees them, known as the Broadcasting Board of Governors (BBG). The rise of this "authoritarian media" phenomenon signals a new stage of political warfare, and a clear challenge to the primacy and clarity of America's standing and message.

For authoritarian powers, information represents a perfect environment in which to test the dominance of U.S. influence that was created during the 20th century. They have seized the technological advantage, working more quickly to utilize social networks, mobile applications, and bot farms to influence and undermine democratic processes in liberal democratic countries, as well as to stifle their own domestic political environments. The result is that USIM today is no longer as dominant a force as it once was in influencing foreign publics, while authoritarian states have gone on the offensive against liberal democratic ideals.

How can and should America respond? There are now signs of welcome change and innovation within the U.S. government, underpinned by a growing understanding among policymakers that USIM is more important than ever to push back against revanchist powers. Thought leaders both inside and outside of government are beginning to rethink the role and structure of USIM to make it better able to confront the propaganda of authoritarian states and actors. Doing so, however, requires understanding where USIM came from, what challenges it now faces, and what goals it hopes to achieve.

COLD WAR ROOTS

The foundations of U.S. public diplomacy and today's U.S. international media were laid in President Franklin Delano Roosevelt's "Good Neighbor" policy toward Latin America during the mid-1930s. Constrained by domestic isolationism and a difficult economy, Roosevelt found that in Latin America he could exercise diplomatic initiative as "a safe passageway between the Scylla of international crisis [in Europe and Asia] and the Charybdis of domestic unilateralism."[2] At the start, public diplomacy was considered a "safe" way to conduct foreign policy, more akin to public relations than a critical tool for great power foreign relations.

Roosevelt and his State Department saw the increasing influence of Germany in Latin America, and looked to America's culture and economy to oppose it. U.S. policymakers recognized that cultural influence "corresponded with the rise and tide of national power" and likened America's use of communications to how the British Empire exported its manufacturing knowledge in the Industrial Age to bind nations to its purposes and needs.[3]

When World War II broke out, these early public diplomacy actions were brought under the war effort as a counter to German propaganda, but still aligned squarely with U.S. democratic ideals and ideas. The Office of War Information (OWI) launched the *Voice of America*, directed toward Germany, on February 1, 1942 with the words, "We bring you Voices from America. Today, and daily from now on, we shall speak to you about America and the war. The news may be good for us. The news may be bad. But we shall tell you the truth."[4]

After World War II, the U.S. quickly dismantled its propaganda operations by decommissioning the OWI and shuttering large portions of the clandestine information programs run by the Office of Strategic Services (OSS), the precursor to today's Central Intelligence Agency. By 1947, a new U.S. policy framework was reshaping America's stance towards the Soviet Union through the Truman Doctrine and the Marshall Plan, animated by George Kennan's theories of "containment" and "counter force."[5] The U.S. recognized that "merely to report the news factually, and to present objectively the policies and practices of the U.S." was no longer enough to address the rising influence of the Soviet Union.[6] Increasingly, America's cold warriors looked to "directly counter Soviet psychological warfare against the U.S.," rather than just point to Soviet vices and U.S. virtues.[7]

The Cold War gave the precursors to what is now called U.S. International Media (USIM) their purpose. The *Voice of America* and subsequently *Radio Free Europe/Radio Liberty* were components of the broad framework envisioned by George Kennan to curtail Soviet expansion in Europe and beyond. Kennan's notion of political warfare included a multi-pronged policy that would block communist expansion in Western Europe and loosen Soviet control in Eastern Europe. It encompassed economic (Marshall Plan), military (NATO), diplomatic and informational elements, as well as overt, covert and activities that fell in between, such as clandestine support of private interest groups to push back on Communist ideology and information programs.

While the Cold War defined the mission of the *Voice of America*, the cultural forces unleashed in the 1960s and beyond set the foundation for the present challenges to the authority and relevance of today's USIM. Where Western advances in broadcast technology enabled the *Voice of America* to be a global news and information channel from the 1950s to the 1990s, the innovation incubated in Silicon Valley fundamentally disrupted the ability of the U.S. to control the speed of information. It was authoritarian countries and non-state actors that first understood the changing ground, and these same elements are now using that advantage to win the first rounds of the 21st century information war.

THE AUTHORITARIANS STRIKE BACK

In the 21st century, information is everywhere. It is embedded in our homes, our hands and even our clothes. The statistics are no longer novel: there are over three billion Internet users, sixty-five percent of the global population is a mobile subscriber, and forty-seven percent of the world's population has an Internet connection.[8] From Berlin to Bamako, people have access to over a billion websites.[9] Digital flows are now responsible for more GDP growth globally than is trade in traditional goods.[10]

In many ways, this new global *milieu* is a product of American success. Western technology, buoyed by Western culture, has been the main driving force for change in recent decades, following the victory of the U.S. in the informational struggle that accompanied the Cold War. From Moscow to Beijing, you can get a cup of coffee at Starbucks, watch a Hollywood movie online and order consumer goods off of Amazon. Yet this cultural and economic dominance has now sparked a counter-revolution, a revival of authoritarianism that is using the culture and technology of the West to reassert undemocratic ideas and modes of governance.

The effectiveness of this revanchist movement is documented in Freedom House's 2018 *Freedom in the World* report, which chronicles the resurgence of the authoritarian state in unflinching language. A key conclusion of the report is that "[d]emocracy faced its most serious crisis in decades in 2017... mark[ing] the 12th consecutive year of decline in global freedom." The report went on to summarize that the U.S. is in retreat as "a champion and an exemplar of democracy amid an accelerating decline in American political rights and civil liberties."[11]

This decline in freedom, and in particular press freedom, is being powered by forces that are undermining and discrediting traditional democratic institutions, including an open and free press. The effects are pronounced. As a recent report by the Rand Corporation documented, American public life is being increasingly affected by growing disagreements over objective truth and declining trust in "formerly respected sources of factual information."[12] And this is happening not only in the United States. The 2018 Edelman Trust Barometer found that, in over sixty percent of countries surveyed, less than fifty percent of respondents expressed trust in government, business, NGOs and the media.[13] It also found that trust among elites was rising, leading to what the survey terms "a grand illusion," or "a lingering notion that elites continue to lead and the masses will follow."[14]

Authoritarian states have used the freedom of the digital age to create a powerful class of information antibodies: the near dominance of opinion over facts, #fakenews, filter bubbles, corrosive memes, phishing, hacking and hate speech. These have become the tools of authoritarian media. A broad array of dictators and authoritarian state and non-state actors are now utilizing Western communication tools – digital and social media, mobile apps and the dark web – to undermine the very civil society that enabled those advances.

The erosion of trust and the rise of opinion is the perfect medium in which to grow authoritarian control. The decade-plus decline in freedom could not have come about without the ability for authoritarian states to aggressively test, improve and evolve media strategies that undermine the relevance and trust in traditional notions of "straight news" and projecting U.S. culture.

In this new media environment, authoritarian states have gone on the offensive to overtly challenge the role and influence of the U.S., and to covertly undermine domestic and international democratic institutions. They realize the potential of technology and the advantage of first-mover propaganda operations, as well as the sophisticated use of modern media tools targeting audience segments, data science and machine learning, along with algorithmic media distribution. They have grasped the significance of modern media and have exploited new opportunities afforded by increasingly sophisticated technology.

By contrast, the United States has been slower to adapt to the 21st century media environment, and U.S. policy has failed to evolve to match the speed of innovation. The U.S. government's information operations are fractured across multiple departments that broadly target national or even regional audiences. Where there is government use of sophisticated technology to analyze media, such as network analysis, machine learning and audience targeting, it has largely been walled off for use by intelligence and national security agencies in their fight against terrorism. And in policy circles, U.S. information strategy is still largely seen as an ancillary tool to explain U.S. policies, rather than a means to lay the groundwork for the success of U.S. goals and actions.

These disadvantages are only amplified within USIM, specifically the Broadcasting Board of Governors and its five sub-networks. The last significant authorization of USIM was the original Smith-Mundt law of 1948 and the *International Broadcasting Act* of 1994/95. While there have been repeated attempts to reform the BBG for the 21st century, these have largely amounted to technical amendments that have set the stage for reform but not implemented any significant or serious change. The result has been an agency that has had neither the authority nor the capabilities to effectively challenge today's revanchist moment.

NEW TACTICS, NEW CHALLENGES

Here, it is important to understand how authoritarian actors gained the advantage, and why it is hard for the U.S. and USIM to push back against their advances. There are three core reasons:

Offense is the new defense

U.S. policymakers have been slow to realize the offensive nature of information war, and too loyal to the traditional notion that U.S. communication platforms are there to "project America" and transmit the decisions of the U.S. government. There is a fundamental misconception by senior U.S. officials that communications come at the tail end of U.S. foreign policy, rather than being used proactively to shape the ground and make policy decisions more successful.

In international relations theory, "offense-dominance" is a concept that helps identify whether the world is unstable and ripe for state conflict, or stable and likely to pacify competing states.[15] The theory holds that when there is no advantage to initiating a war first (the offensive position) and defending against attack is actually more advantageous, the world is generally stable. In contrast, if there is a strategic advantage to being the "first-mover" and adopting an offensive position – and especially if the offensive position is more affordable than defensive countermeasures – there is conflict. This concept is now playing out in the information wars of the modern digital age.[16]

At its core are the central changes to media competition ushered in by the Internet and mobile networks. Digital media has made propaganda distribution accessible, cheap, and practically impossible to eliminate due to the decentralized and redundant nature of the Internet, mobile apps and social networks. This point is even more worrisome as increasingly powerful commercial ad-based technology, machine learning and statistical sampling enable propagandists to target a message to small-group audiences. They mask their messages within the rising tide of opinion and use the power of humor and outrage to build a familiarity and relevance with the audience.

Psychological operations are not new. Modern "psyops" are the result of social science research of the early 20th century, and such techniques were embedded in military structures as long ago as World War I. Even so, Russia's recent successes in weaponizing information stand out. Kremlin leaders clearly appreciate the power of the media, and have excelled at its application in the 21st century.[17] Russia's use of information operations has been highly aggressive, tactical and increasingly public, thanks to the dedication of investigative journalists. But other repressive states have likewise developed subtle, strategic programs designed to generate doubt and promote "non-interference" from foreign powers as they pursue their interests. For these actors, offense has become the best defense against the destabilizing potential of the liberal order and Western values.

Small, agile and aggressive

Information war has gone through a transformation from large powerful broadcasters radiating a central message to small agile groups that can segment, target and engage audiences with messages that reflect their micro-values. For instance, when the Russians operationalized information warfare and propaganda, they did so through a quasi-private sector operation in St. Petersburg known as the Internet Research Agency.[18] This "troll farm" first focused on undermining the ideological enemies of the Kremlin, building support for Russian President Vladimir Putin and laying the foundations for foreign operations by attacking the image of Western leaders such as President Barack Obama and German Chancellor Angela Merkel.

Other states are investing in such "forward-deployed" information forces as well. From Iran's cyber jihadists to China's numerous media and cyber centers,[19] authoritarian actors are using overseas operations to attack perceived enemies, and harnessing tactics like "hashtag poisoning" to disrupt undesirable conversation or drown opposing messages in internet "noise."[20] But the cutting edge in small, agile and flexible information units are those pioneered the Islamic State terrorist group (ISIS), which knows how to use media technologies deftly to produce content that is relevant, localized, and targeted to segmented audiences. The audience-first approach taken by ISIS in content creation, distribution, and engagement, and its nodes of dedicated, "professional" propagandists who create model content and inspire propaganda[21] in turn may point to how authoritarian states may organize their future operations.

The increasingly global phenomenon of #Fakenews

America's most visible communicator, President Donald Trump, has become notorious for his use of social media as a political instrument. But the president's adroit "counter punching" at his domestic opponents has global ramifications. In particular, his penchant to broadly label all news content deemed undesirable, irrespective of its veracity, as "fake news" has had a material – and detrimental – impact upon the credibility of the media in the eyes of the American people. As Freedom House has documented, it has also contributed to the perception that the U.S. is retreating from its commitment to an open and free press.[22]

This approach, in turn, has been taken up by other leaders (from Venezuelan President Nicolas Maduro to Turkey's Recep Tayyip Erdogan), who have attempted to discredit the media as a way of justifying or obscuring their own actions.[23] The inherent danger in this dynamic is that it helps to cultivate opposition to a free, vibrant and independent press, and contributes to the goal of increased political control of the media that is embraced by authoritarian regimes. The core challenge for USIM is that the President's statements are amplified by the propaganda of authoritarian states in order to undermine U.S. influence.

NAVIGATING THE NEW ENVIRONMENT

In this environment, USIM is facing its gravest challenge since the Cold War. USIM is challenged by increased media competition, the agility of authoritarian states to adapt their domestic markets to new ways of information control and censorship, and by the way in which traditional U.S. democratic ideals have been undermined domestically and abroad.

Today, according to the U.S. government's own estimates, the combined organs of American public diplomacy reach over 278 million viewers and listeners.[24] Crucially, however, those audiences are not solely their own. Rather, a number of authoritarian states have launched new broadcast and digital media operations (among them *Russia Today*, *CCTV*, *Al Jazeera* and *Press TV*) in a bid to capture and contest media audiences. Beyond these new actors, a whole new arena of media competition has emerged – one that in which non-state actors like ISIS and quasi-state media organizations like Russia's Internet Research Agency are active, and in which non-attributable automated information warfare capabilities (such as computational propaganda, bot farms and malware) are being used to great effect.

Authoritarian media is enjoying unprecedented success today because its wielders have learned three fundamental lessons of the current international environment. The first is that offense is more effective than defense, as trust in traditional institutions wanes and opinion trumps fact. The second is that focused, agile communicators can use advanced technology to capture a powerful advantage and deliver highly focused messages. Finally, authoritarian regimes have learned that they can effectively manage their domestic media environments with a mixture of censorship and nationalism to dull outside influences.

Fundamentally, political warfare in the 21st century is centered on a struggle for cohesion. For revanchist powers, such as the Kremlin and Iran's clerical regime, the aim is to undermine the liberal democratic order and the institutions that govern it. For rising powers, such as China, the goal is to create cohesion by drawing together other authoritarian powers in a network of trade, technology and policy, as well as to break the grip of global institutions that do not reflect their values. Authoritarian powers and non-state actors are using instability as a force multiplier to break Western cohesion. The tactics they use are allowing them to play a more powerful hand than their economies, military, technological sophistication or culture would otherwise allow.

The role of USIM, by contrast, is to foster long-term strategic cohesion of the liberal democratic order, and to be the conduit that invites the global audience to join, participate in and enjoy the benefits of that order. The USIM system – the Broadcasting Board of Governors and the individual networks and services it oversees – is America's most powerful platform in this effort. In order for it to be successful today, however, USIM will need to be reoriented to accomplish several concrete goals.

Shaping media markets

At their most ambitious, the capabilities of USIM can be melded with other elements of the U.S. government – most notably USAID and the State Department – to influence the evolution of global media markets in ways that undermine the effectiveness of authoritarian media, propaganda and information operations. In rapidly expanding media markets in Africa and Asia (and to a lesser extent, Latin America), the U.S. can expand its provision of technical assistance and support to media regulatory bodies that ensure open competition. At its core, these efforts should be underpinned by the understanding that, now more than ever, the U.S. needs to make the promotion of free and open media markets a key element of its trade policy, and a core principle in its national security calculations.

Fortunately, America possesses potent tools to assist in this effort. The United States is home to some of the most powerful communication platform companies in the world. This group includes not only the obvious heavyweights like Facebook, Twitter and YouTube, but also companies that operate at the more fundamental layers of information distribution: search platforms (Google, Yahoo, Microsoft), cloud service companies (Amazon AWS, Microsoft), content distribution networks (Akamai, Rackspace), fiber networks (CenturyLink, AT&T, Verizon) and assorted other mobile, cable and other telecommunication companies. Casting the net more broadly, the U.S. is the home of or a significant market share for the large digital advertising agencies (Edelman, Group M, WPP) and core advertisers that support global media networks. This gives the United States tremendous informal power to align the interests of platforms, applications and digital advertising channels to support open media, while also limiting the access and activities of bad actors, both state and nonstate.

This is already beginning to happen, as evidenced by the growing role of private sector companies and digital platforms, including Google's in-house think tank, Jigsaw, and YouTube, to limit the scope and reach of radical messaging by the Islamic State.[25] Assuming such a proactive role in their approach to authoritarian media outlets should be encouraged among a broad range of actors who are not yet engaged in today's "battle of ideas."

Fostering 21st century institutions

There is a strong rationale for building or supporting new institutions that support liberal democratic values which are built (or born) for the information age of the 21st century. Such institutions are already emerging. From businesses such as Kiva, which connects entrepreneurs to capital and technical support, to Start-up Weekend and Mobile Mondays (both examples of high-tech networking), a new breed of networked institutions is beginning to coalesce, empowered by the new global media environment to engage in the fields of sustainability, education, science, culture and human rights.

The role of USIM should be to invest in these organizations by promoting participation in them, celebrating their successes and partnering with them to create media platforms that enable members to connect, share and collaborate. The success of such networks will not only build strong, resilient people-to-people connections, but also act as a conduit for the transmission of liberal democratic ideals. If such organizations are recognized as assets, a reconstituted USIM could partner with this growing ecosystem to form the foundation of a new generation of institutions capable of resisting revanchist forces.

Engaged audiences

In order to be successful, USIM must focus its efforts not just on messaging broadly, but on connecting concretely with key strategic audiences. Counterintuitive as it may seem, USIM needs to take a lesson from authoritarian states, and particularly from non-state actors such as ISIS, in the way those entities skillfully segment and target audiences. This is common practice in sophisticated commercial media and advertising, but it has not, to date, been utilized effectively by the organs of USIM. While the BBG has begun to harness modern research techniques, there is still a lack of the skilled staff needed to power this approach. Simply put, USIM needs data scientists, community managers, developers and social marketers to more adroitly use open and closed platforms to target key audiences.

Engagement is not just about targeting audiences, however. It is also about building a relationship with viewers/listeners/readers based on an exchange of value between both parties. A key advantage of globalization and the growth of digital networks has been to expand access to information. Opportunities now exist for audiences not only to come together around problems, but also to take concrete action to solve them.

By targeting and engaging key audiences, the U.S. can leverage the comparative advantage afforded by it 21st century information economy and open culture. USIM is still the most effective public tool available to the United States to increase the credibility and relevance of the American experience – including open, passionate discussions about issues that impact liberal Western democracy. By showing how we succeed, how we fail, and how we engage on issues ranging from race to politics to societal equality, America can demonstrate by example that openness and debate make us stronger.

ADAPTING THE ARCHITECTURE

However, USIM's role in shaping today's media markets, and in supporting the next generation of institutions and engage with contemporary audiences, requires significant structural reform and reauthorization. The BBG is an institution that has its foundations in the Cold War. Its muscles for 21st century innovation are under-utilized and in an uneasy alliance with more traditional broadcasting technology, workflows and mentalities. In order for smart reform to happen, U.S. policymakers must focus on three key goals.

The first is that the BBG must *rebalance* its approach. It must move away from almost exclusively creating news and information through its own services, and expand its support for an array of content types and content producers. While news is an essential tool, it is not the only one. Essential new programming must be generated by aiding the formation of people-to-people networks of entrepreneurs, artists, community builders and political activists. The role of USIM should be not just to create content, but to facilitate the production and distribution of content from independent and investigative journalists and documentarians, as well as to provide production assistance to nonprofits, foundations and democratic activists in the creation of high-quality, active and engaging work.

The second goal is to *transition* into a sophisticated digital organization. At its core, this requires the BBG to attract and retain staff who have the relevant skills to match fast-evolving media markets. By necessity, such a cadre would include journalists with updated skill sets, as well as social media marketing specialists, those knowledgeable about data science and experienced digital producers and distribution managers. This new workforce needs to be as close to the creation, production and distribution of content as possible.

It also means speeding the evolution of the BBG's distribution channels into digital platforms from which key target audiences receive their information. The era of effective shortwave broadcasting has come to a close, and that of satellite broadcasting has peaked. But the new era of tunneling through Internet firewalls and inserting media into censored social networks has only just begun. The structure of the BBG needs to adapt accordingly, with the old newsroom model broken up into smaller, flexible and purpose-built content units. (Good examples of such an approach are *RFE/RL*'s recently launched Polygraph unit, which fact-checks disinformation and misinformation in the Russian press, and *Current Time*, a set of dedicated news programs for Russian speakers in the

Baltics and Eastern Europe.)

The last goal is *organizational reform* of the BBG and its networks into a single media company under a single CEO. Just as the BBG as a whole needs to move to more flexible, purpose-built content units, the CEO's core goal would be to enable a more aggressive forward deployment of USIM units closer to, and where they can be more connected with, the audience. This could include the production of content in, or near, priority markets, as well as the creation of units that commission relevant local content tied to advancing liberal democratic outcomes.

Any such changes, however, need to be driven by a larger understanding. Political warfare is now being fought in the ether of social media and cyberspace. The BBG needs to participate in this fast-paced change, not only to inoculate audiences against propaganda, but to go on the offensive by engaging and recruiting audiences to align themselves with Western values. Authoritarian media players have the initiative, and have organized themselves around a sophisticated playbook. They have a keen appreciation of the hopes and fears of their audiences and are relentlessly targeting them via the smart, strategic use of technology. In order to push back successfully, USIM needs to reform, reorganize, reorient and redefine itself for the 21st Century.

ENDNOTES

1. As cited in Scott Lucas, *Freedom's War: The US Crusade Against the Soviet Union, 1945-56* (Manchester University Press, 1999), 132.
2. Justin Hart, *Empire of Ideas: The Origins of Public Diplomacy and the Transformation of U.S. Foreign Policy* (Oxford University Press, 2013), 20.
3. Ibid.,. 50.
4. Voice of America, "VOA Through The Years," n.d., https://www.insidevoa.com/a/3794247.html.
5. Lowell Schwartz, *Political Warfare Against the Kremlin: US and British Policy at the Beginning of the Cold War* (Palgrave MacMillan, 2009), 96 - 123.
6. Hart, *Empire of Ideas*, 130.
7. U.S. Department of State, "Report to the President by the National Security Council 20/4," n.d., https://history.state.gov/historical-documents/frus1948v01p2/d60.
8. GSMA, "GSMA Mobile Economy 2018," n.d., https://www.gsma.com/mobileeconomy/.
9. Stephanie Pappas, "How Big is the Internet, Really?" *LiveScience*, March 18, 2016, https://www.livescience.com/54094-how-big-is-the-internet.html.
10. McKinsey Global Institute, "Digital Globalization: The New Era of Global Flows," March 2016, https://www.mckinsey.com/~/media/McKinsey/Business%20Functions/McKinsey%20Digital/Our%20Insights/Digital%20globalization%20The%20new%20era%20of%20global%20flows/MGI-Digital-globalization-Full-report.ashx.
11. Freedom House, *Freedom in the World 2018: Democracy in Crisis* (Freedom House, 2018), https://freedomhouse.org/report/freedom-world/freedom-world-2018.
12. Jennifer Kavanagh and Michael D. Rich, *Truth Decay: An Initial Exploration of the Diminishing Role of Facts and Analysis in American Public Life* (Rand Corporation, 2018), 57.
13. Edelman, *Edelman Trust Barometer Global Report 2018*, n.d., http://cms.edelman.com/sites/default/files/2018-02/2018_Edelman_Trust_Barometer_Global_Report_FEB.pdf.
14. Edelman, *Edelman Trust Barometer Global Report 2016*, n.d., https://www.edelman.com/research/2016-trust-barometer-executive-summary.

15. Stephen Van Evera, *Causes of War: Power and the Roots of Conflict* (Ithaca: Cornell UP, 1999), 117-92.

16. Robert Bole and Kevin Kallmyer, "Combatting the Islamic State's Digital Dominance: Revitalizing U.S. Communication Strategy," *The Washington Quarterly* 39, iss. 1, 2016, 29-48.

17. General Valery Gerasimov, the current Chief of the General Staff of the Russian Federation, has written that "The role of nonmilitary means of achieving political and strategic goals has grown, and, in many cases, they have exceeded the power of force of weapons in their effectiveness." He goes on to discuss how information warfare is not just the province of state actors, but that it would be well understood that "internal opposition [could] create a permanently operating front through the entire territory of the enemy state." See Mark Galeotti, "The 'Gerasimov Doctrine' and Russian Non-Linear War," *In Moscow's Shadows*, July 6, 2014, https://inmoscowsshadows.wordpress.com/2014/07/06/the-gerasimov-doctrine-and-russian-non-linear-war/#more-2291.

18. Dmitry Volchek and Daisy Sindelar, "One Professional Russian Troll Tells All," *Radio Free Europe/Radio Liberty*, March 25, 2015, https://www.rferl.org/a/how-to-guide-russian-trolling-trolls/26919999.html.

19. Yuan Yang, "China's Communist party raises army of nationalist trolls," *Financial Times*, December 29, 2017, https://www.ft.com/content/9ef9f592-e2bd-11e7-97e2-916d4fbac0da.

20. Freedom House, *Press Freedom's Dark Horizon, Freedom of the Press 2017* (Freedom House, 2017), https://freedomhouse.org/report/freedom-net/2017/saudi-arabia.

21. For an excellent summative history of IS's media operations, see Craig Whiteside, "Lighting the Path: the evolution of the Islamic State Media Enterprise (2003 - 2016)," ICCT *Research Paper*, November 2016, https://icct.nl/wp-content/uploads/2016/11/ICCT-Whiteside-Lighting-the-Path-the-Evolution-of-the-Islamic-State-Media-Enterprise-2003-2016-Nov2016.pdf.

22. Freedom House, *Press Freedom's Dark Horizon, Freedom of the Press 2017*.

23. Krishnadev Calamur, "From Trump's Twitter Feed to Dictators' Mouths," *The Atlantic*, December 14, 2010, https://www.theatlantic.com/international/archive/2017/12/trump-fake-news-dictators/548414/.

24. Broadcasting Board of Governors, "BBG Global Audience Estimate

From the FY 2017 Performance and Results Report, n.d., https://www.bbg.gov/strategy-and-performance/performance-accountability/.

25. For a detailed overview of such efforts, see Robert Bole, "Western Technology vs. Extremism," AFPC *Defense Dossier* iss. 18, December 2016, http://www.afpc.org/files/defense_dossier_december_issue_18.pdf.

CONCLUSION
RESPONDING TO AUTHORITARIAN MEDIA
Ilan Berman

Today, the danger that authoritarian media poses to the United States is growing, as more and more hostile actors embrace the strategic use of information and propaganda to solidify their domestic position and advance their foreign policy objectives.

At home, the proliferation of foreign disinformation and "fake news" has threatened the integrity of America's media sphere, contributed to an erosion of public trust in U.S. media institutions, and helped to shape the opinions of citizens in ways beneficial to authoritarian actors – and detrimental to democracy. Abroad, the competitive advantage enjoyed by American outreach throughout most of the 20th century is steadily diminishing, as authoritarians exploit the very things that historically afforded advantage and resonance to the U.S. message (among them the openness of media markets and innovations in communications technology) to promote their own message, obscure objective truth, and dilute democratic processes.

Global opinion, in other words, can no longer be considered an uncontested environment. In order to maintain its dominant position in this increasingly competitive milieu, the United States will need to make major upgrades to the structure, function and prominence of its own messaging – as well as to affect changes in how it approaches this unfolding arena of competition at home.

UPGRADING AMERICA'S ARGUMENT

For decades, U.S. public outreach has been guided by the principle propounded in 1963 by Edward R. Murrow: that, by its nature, truthful, objective journalism is sufficient to sway world publics and global public opinion to America's cause. That may have been true during the decades of the Cold War, when U.S. and Western free media provided a potent antidote to the closed societies and heavy-handed censors of the Soviet bloc. Today, however, a compelling case can be made that we have entered a "post-Murrow moment" – one in which the traditional principles of U.S. strategic communication are being sorely tested by the rise of authoritarian media and the proliferation of new technologies and platforms which have afforded hostile actors far greater media reach. The United States must, therefore, do likewise, and improve its ability to engage and persuade foreign publics while simultaneously discrediting and marginalizing authoritarian actors.

This is hardly a call to adopt the methods of disinformation favored by Vladimir Putin's Russia, or to embrace the missionary ideological media of Iran's ayatollahs. Far from it. Rather, it requires the United States to marry its enduring message about freedom and democracy with an embrace of new technologies and a far greater familiarity with the contemporary platforms (such as social media) most effective in disseminating those messages.

During the 1930s, the infamous bank robber Willie Sutton gained national notoriety in the United States for a string of daring heists in New York and Philadelphia. When he was apprehended by law enforcement authorities, they asked him why banks were his targets of choice. Sutton is famously said to have answered, "because that's where the money is." Like Willie Sutton, America today needs to go "where the money is" in its messaging, and erect a much more robust presence in the digital domain. The reasons are obvious; today, more than half of the world's population (just over four billion people) are active Internet users, while more than forty percent (3.19 billion people) maintain an active presence on social media.[1] Unless the United States engages more fully with these publics in their domains of choice, it runs the risk of having its message eclipsed by those who do.

Effective media competition, however, will require more than simply changing the focus and platforms of our messaging. It likewise necessitates upgrades to the architecture of America's instruments of influence.[2]

In the opening stages of the Cold War, the United States laid the groundwork for a formidable informational bureaucracy designed to wage a war of ideas with the Soviet Union, with the goal of reducing "the power and influence of the Kremlin inside the Soviet Union and other areas under its control."[3] In the decades that followed, this effort gave rise to new government structures and authorities to carry out strategic influence operations – from psychological warfare to propaganda – during peacetime. In turn, the advent of the Reagan administration brought with it a comprehensive strategic effort to defeat the Soviet Union and roll back Soviet ideology. U.S. public diplomacy was a big part of this plan, and successive presidential directives during the 1980s expanded the number, scope and reach of America's broadcasting instruments as part of an extensive strategic communications campaign to "counter totalitarian ideologies and aggressive political action moves undertaken by the Soviet Union or Soviet surrogates."[4] Their work has been credited by experts as playing a key role in successfully winning the Cold War for the West.

Following the end of the Cold War and the USSR's demise, however, U.S. officials embarked upon a systematic dismantlement of the informational infrastructure that had so successfully communicated American values and ideals to the captive masses behind the Iron Curtain. Throughout the 1990s, U.S. strategic communications suffered death by a thousand cuts, as important and dynamic programs were progressively eliminated, funding for them dwindled, and the human brain trust that had helped to win the ideological battle against Soviet Communism dispersed. The crowning blow came in October of 1999, when the United States Information Agency (USIA) – which until then had served as the operational nerve center of U.S. public outreach – was formally folded into the State Department as part of new legislation aimed at restructuring and streamlining the nation's public diplomacy effort.

In place of the USIA, the U.S. government erected a hybrid structure, part bureaucratic and part programmatic, to oversee American outreach. Formally, the U.S. State Department took charge of the country's public affairs, cultural outreach and international education efforts. Practically, American broadcasting became the bailiwick of the Broadcasting Board of Governors (BBG), a government agency overseen by a bipartisan panel of congressionally-appointed businessmen and media figures. The overall effect was deeply detrimental to the cohesiveness of American messaging. Strategic vision has atrophied, with the BBG and its employees at times seeing themselves as separate from – and not beholden to – U.S. policy,[5] while strategic communications became relegated to a second-tier policy priority, with assets scattered across the federal bureaucracy.

In the nearly two decades since, scores of studies have taken stock of America's diminished post-Cold War ability to exert strategic influence abroad, and proffered suggestions about how the United States can best reorganize to compete on the contemporary informational battlefield.[6] While their recommendations differ, the larger message underpinning these assessments is unanimous: the United States needs more capabilities, greater investments and above all a coherent vision in order to effectively wage the "war of ideas" in the 21st century.

Such change is now happening – albeit slowly. Since the advent of the Trump administration, the bureaucracy of the BBG, long resistant to implementing serious changes in the way it does business, has been spurred into action. Worried over the potential consequences of continuing to do "business as usual," the BBG has begun to make much-needed upgrades to its broadcasting and outreach to key countries of foreign policy concern.

Thus, following an in-depth independent assessment of U.S. Persian-language media (spearheaded by this author),[7] the agency has started to implement significant improvements to the quality and content of its outreach to Iran. The most notable of these is a recently unveiled plan to launch a new, 24/7 Farsi-language channel dedicated to more deeply engaging with Iranians across broadcast, digital and social media platforms early in 2019.[8] American broadcasting toward Russia and the "post-Soviet space," too, has received much-needed attention since Russia's invasion of Ukraine in 2014, including through the 2017 launch of "Current Time," a 24/7 Russian-language worldwide TV and digital network, and the creation of Polygraph.info, an English-language website dedicated to fact-checking and debunking Russian disinformation.

The bureaucracy of U.S. outreach itself is changing as well. Since 2014, Congressional advocates have repeatedly attempted to mandate structural changes to U.S. public diplomacy.[9] But time and again, such steps failed as standalone measures, ultimately prompting the decision to fold them into broader legislation. The result was the addition of amendments dedicated to reform of the BBG to the 2017 *National Defense Authorization Act*, which President Barack Obama signed into law in December 2016. An overhaul of U.S. public diplomacy has thus become a matter of law – although the exact pace of this change remains unclear. As of this writing, a new Chief Executive Officer has been formally nominated by the Trump administration to replace current BBG chief John Lansing. At some point in the future, the BBG's governing board will also become defunct, replaced by an advisory panel that is smaller in size and beholden to the new CEO.[10] The logic underpinning these changes is clear: in order to make American outreach more competitive, its management needs to become more streamlined, and the inherent inefficiencies that have long plagued U.S. public diplomacy need to be removed. And if our informational adversaries are increasingly operating as start-ups, the thinking goes, American strategic communications should as well.

Whether such changes will end up being salutary, however, remains to be seen. This is because an overhaul of BBG management carries with it the risk of derailing, or at least temporarily stalling, the reforms and upgrades now underway within the agency. Likewise, the transition of the BBG to a less transparent, more vertically organized agency may make it more difficult for overseers in the Executive Branch and Congress to accurately gauge the effectiveness and integrity of its inner workings. Nevertheless, the changes now underway to the content and structure of U.S. public diplomacy are a long-overdue recognition that the international informational environment has changed, and that America's message and posture must change with it.

REGULATION, AND ITS LIMITS

The extensive attempts by Russian actors to subvert the U.S. media in the run-up to the 2016 presidential election have given rise to a new national conversation about the extent to which the U.S. government should intervene in the country's "marketplace of ideas." Such a discussion is unprecedented in American politics; historically, the U.S. government adopted a mostly *laissez faire* attitude toward the "Fourth Estate," imposing only marginal constraints (and then mostly based around restrictions against obscenity and indecency[11]) on the assorted media conglomerates and broadcasting outlets, both foreign and domestic, operating within the United States, in deference to the freedom of speech provisions embedded in the First Amendment. But the rise of authoritarian media, and the proliferation of malign actors throughout the U.S. media marketplace, has increasingly challenged this historically lax attitude, and spurred the Trump administration into action.

Thus, in the Fall of 2017, the U.S. Justice Department ordered Russia's flagship English-language channel, *RT*, to formally register as a foreign agent pursuant to the 1938 *Foreign Agents Registration Act* (FARA).[12] The requirement drew angry denunciations from *RT*'s editor-in-chief, Margarita Simonyan, who termed the requirement "illegitimate."[13] Nevertheless, the broadcaster grudgingly complied in order to continue its operations in the United States. (Similar requirements were subsequently leveled on Russia's *Sputnik* multimedia platform.)

What does this mean, as a practical matter? Official Kremlin protestations notwithstanding, FARA requirements have not restricted access to the U.S. media market for Russian entities. *RT*, like other foreign broadcasters (including the BBC and France24), remains free to broadcast its content to American audiences, and does so actively. However, pursuant to FARA, *RT* and Sputnik now need to label their content with disclaimers that disclose foreign funding and make clear that they operate on behalf of a foreign power.[14] Designation thus reflects an effort by U.S. authorities to better arm American media consumers with the information necessary to critically absorb the messages that are being propounded by these entities.

RT's designation provides an important early precedent for how the U.S. government can and should approach other examples of authoritarian media and malign informational actors in the future. After all, the number of authoritarian media sources within the U.S. market has increased exponentially in recent years, and now includes not only *RT* and *Sputnik*, but also China's *CCTV*, Qatar's *Al-Jazeera* and a host of other outlets that promote narratives and discourse which are at times diametrically opposed to American values. Publicly identifying these entities, and forcing them to operate more transparently, represents an important step in insulating the American public from foreign propaganda and disinformation.

Such a policy needs to be applied uniformly, however. So far, the U.S. government's approach to authoritarian media has been ad hoc in nature. It has failed to follow clearly defined guidelines regarding which foreign broadcasters should be forced to register under FARA, and why. This has brought the Administration in for deserved criticism from watchdog groups, which have decried the lack of clear standards for censure, and the resulting appearance of selective political bias.[15] Thus, while a compelling policy case can be made regarding the need to extend FARA registration requirements to other foreign media actors, doing so in practice will require the U.S. government to develop and promulgate clearly set criteria for designation – so that foreign outlets have standards to follow in their operations, and so that there can be no doubt about the penalties if they fail to abide by them.

A second emerging area of government regulation resides in the social media sphere. Much of Russia's disinformation campaign against the United States to date has taken place on Facebook and other social media platforms. Other authoritarian actors, most conspicuously the Islamic State, have actively exploited this arena as well, harnessing Google,

YouTube and Telegram to disseminate their messages. The focus is logical; because of its newness and dynamism, social media has operated absent meaningful regulation, with governments relying on the companies themselves to police content and users. This, in turn, has left the medium vulnerable to exploitation by agile and technologically-savvy hostile actors.

This vulnerability has, of late, become the subject of intense scrutiny on Capitol Hill. In the wake of revelations that British data firm Cambridge Analytica mined personal information from Facebook users for political purposes, Congress convened a series of hearings in the Spring of 2018 to assess the corporate practices, privacy safeguards and vulnerabilities of that company, and others. As a result of that inquiry, there is now a broad consensus among U.S. lawmakers, at least in principle, that the burgeoning domain of social media requires greater regulation.[16] But as a practical matter, concrete measures to better regulate and protect the social media sphere still remain largely conceptual, hamstrung by partisan politics and the opacity of social media platforms themselves. Nevertheless, as even Facebook CEO Mark Zuckerberg has acknowledged, greater government regulation of – and oversight over – digital companies and platforms is "inevitable."[17] Indeed, how to do so is now the subject of active policy debate, with various regulatory models under active consideration (among them the concept that social media should be treated in much the same way as utilities such as electricity and water.) Whatever path is ultimately chosen, U.S. policymakers will need to work to ensure that social media platforms remain both pluralistic (providing for a diversity of political views) and secure, adopting corporate practices that reduce social media's attractiveness to authoritarian actors, and its vulnerability to exploitation by them.

THE LESSON FOR AMERICAN MEDIA

No discussion of the phenomenon of authoritarian media would be complete without at least some mention of the milieu in which it has arguably proven to be most effective: U.S. domestic media. Indeed, the current fragmentation and volatility visible in the American media landscape has made it increasingly susceptible to exploitation by foreign forces, much to the detriment of democratic principles and the integrity of the country's institutions.

At their most constructive, the scope, reach and resources of

America's media outlets position them as a potent antidote to the proliferation of "fake news" and disinformation by authoritarian actors. Yet
the credibility of the U.S. media is now in question as never before. While
politicization and bias in America's media corporations has long been
a pervasive problem,[18] the advent of the Trump era has exacerbated the
challenge dramatically. The controversial nature of the 2016 presidential
election, and many of the polarizing decisions made by the Administration since, have garnered extensive negative coverage from the U.S. press
– coverage which has often come at the expense of journalistic credibility.
Repeated instances of poor journalistic practices, from improper political shading to the outright fabrication of stories,[19] have contributed to
the belief among many Americans that the national media is hopelessly
biased, unrepresentative and politically driven. They have also made it
much easier for the Administration to discount and denigrate negative
stories as "fake news," notwithstanding their actual merit.

Reclaiming national trust requires America's media institutions
to reposition themselves as impartial and credible communicators of objective truth. This does not mean a diminution of the media's coverage of
the Administration actions and policies. Historically, the "Fourth Estate"
has played an essential role in the democratic process, including by exposing (and thereby limiting) the excesses of successive administrations.
But in today's polarized political climate, extra care must be taken by U.S.
media outlets to ensure greater rigor, transparency and credibility in their
reporting. If they do not, their integrity will continue to suffer, creating an
opening in American public opinion that authoritarian media actors can
and will exploit.

A WAR FOR OPINION

The U.S. government is now giving serious thought to the evolving nature of conflict in the 21st century, and the need for greater strategic capabilities in order to compete in – and dominate – multiple domains.[20] Increasingly, global opinion must be considered such an arena
of competition. In the years ahead, we should fully expect authoritarian
media to make America's efforts to engage foreign constituencies more
and more difficult, as publics in various countries are bombarded with
massive, and often misleading, media "noise" designed to steer them
away from meaningful engagement with democratic processes or to "tune

out" altogether. At the same time, strategic messaging from repressive regimes will seek to undermine freedom and democratic principles in ways that adversely affect the global standing of the United States and its Western partners.

In this evolving competition, Russia may be the most visible culprit, but it is hardly the only one. As Secretary of Defense James Mattis told graduates at the United States Naval Academy in June of 2018, the Kremlin today "aims to diminish the appeal of the Western democratic model and attempts to undermine America's moral authority" through actions that "are designed not to challenge our arms, but to undercut and compromise our belief in our ideals."[21] That description can increasingly be applied to the Chinese Communist Party, Iran's clerical regime, and the digital radicals of the Islamic State as well. As the preceding pages outline, authoritarian media has become a truly global phenomenon, embraced by regimes from Moscow to Doha as a way of improving their strategic position, and diminishing that of their ideological competitors – chief among them the United States.

The resulting challenge is daunting, but meeting it is vital to U.S. security. As recent events have made abundantly clear, forging a strategic response to authoritarian media will be essential to maintaining the primacy of America's global message, and preserving the international resonance of democratic principles, in the 21st century.

ENDNOTES

1. Simon Kemp, "Digital in 2018: World's Internet Users Pass the 4 Billion Mark," *We Are Social* blog, January 30, 2018, https://wearesocial.com/uk/blog/2018/01/global-digital-report-2018.
2. The following section contains passages drawn from the author's earlier book, *Winning the Long War: Retaking the Offensive Against Radical Islam* (Rowman & Littlefield, 2009). They are reproduced here with the publisher's permission.
3. White House, National Security Council, *NSC 68: United States Objectives and Programs for National Security*, April 14, 1950, http://www.fas.org/irp/offdocs/nsc-hst/nsc-68.htm.
4. In July of 1982, the Reagan administration issued National Security Decision Directive 45, which expanded the role of the *Voice of America* and *Radio Free Europe/Radio Liberty* (RFE/RL), and created a new initiative, known as *Radio Marti*, aimed at assisting the destabilization and discrediting of Fidel Castro's Cuba. See White House, *National Security Decision Directive* 45, "United States International Broadcasting," July 15, 1982, http://www.fas.org/irp/offdocs/nsdd/nsdd-045.htm. Subsequently, in January of 1983, these efforts were combined into a comprehensive strategic effort with the passage of NSDD 77, which became the Reagan administration's comprehensive strategy to defeat the USSR. White House, *National Security Decision Directive* 77, "Management of Public Diplomacy Relative to National Security," January 14, 1983. (author's collection)
5. As one Board member famously put it back in 2002, "We've got to think of ourselves as separate from public diplomacy." Edward Kaufman, as cited in Glenn Hauser, ed., *DX Listening Digest* 2-142, September 11, 2002, http://www.worldofradio.com/dxld2142.txt.
6. These include, among many others, *Finding America's Voice: A Strategy for Reinvigorating U.S. Public Diplomacy*, (New York: Council on Foreign Relations, 2003); Stephen Johnson and Helle Dale, "How to Reinvigorate U.S. Public Diplomacy," Heritage Foundation Backgrounder no. 1645, April 2003; *Changing Minds, Winning Peace: A New Strategic Direction for U.S. Public Diplomacy in the Arab & Muslim World* (Washington: Advisory Group on Public Diplomacy for the Arab and Muslim World, October 1, 2003,) U.S. Department of Defense, Office of the Under Secretary of Defense for

Acquisition, Technology and Logistics, *Report of the Defense Science Board Task Force on Strategic Communication*, September 2004; J. Michael Waller, *Fighting the War of Ideas Like a Real War* (Washington, DC: Institute of World Politics Press, 2007); and Douglas J. Feith, William A. Galston, and Abram N. Shulsky, "Organizing for a Strategic Ideas Campaign to Counter Ideological Challenges to U.S. National Security," Hudson Institute *Security & Foreign Affairs Briefing Paper*, April 2012, http://www.dougfeith.com/docs/2012_04_Feith_Galston_Shulsky_Paper.pdf.

7. American Foreign Policy Council, "U.S. Persian Media Study: Final Synthesis Report," October 6, 2017, https://www.bbg.gov/wp-content/media/2011/11/AFPC_Persian-Language-Broadcasting-Study_synthesis-report.pdf.

8. The formal announcement of the new channel was made by BBG CEO John Lansing at a May 29, 2018 conference at the Hudson Institute on media and politics in Iran. Video of the event, including Lansing's remarks, is available here: https://www.hudson.org/events/1564-a-challenging-crossroad-media-and-politics-in-iran52018.

9. Most prominently, in May of 2015, Cong. Edward Royce (R-CA) and Eliot Engel (D-NY) introduced the *United States International Communications Reform Act* with the goal of creating a dedicated new informational bureaucracy to manage U.S. international outreach in lieu of the BBG. See House Foreign Affairs Committee, "H.R. 2323, United States International Communications Reform Act of 2015, SECTION-BY-SECTION SUMMARY," 2015, https://foreignaffairs.house.gov/files/BBG%20Reform%20section-by-section.pdf.

10. See Broadcasting Board of Governors, "Technical Amendments to the International Broadcasting Act," n.d., https://www.bbg.gov/who-we-are/oversight/legislation/technical-amendments-international-broadcasting-act/.

11. These include the George W. Bush administration's passage, in 2006, of the *Broadcast Decency Enforcement Act*, which significantly increased fines for violations of Federal Communications Commission standards for broadcast content. See Jim Abrams, "Congress Increases Indecency Fines Tenfold," Washington Post, June 7, 2006, http://www.washingtonpost.com/wp-dyn/content/article/2006/06/07/AR2006060701790_pf.html.

12. Hadas Gold, "Russia's RT America Registers with DOJ as a Foreign Agent," *CNN*, November 13, 2017, http://money.cnn.com/2017/11/13/media/russia-rt-fara/index.html.

13. "RT Editor-In-Chief Calls US Demand on Registration Under FARA Illegitimate," *Sputnik*, September 30, 2017, https://sputniknews.com/us/201709301057828905-rt-usa-foreign-agent-registration-illegitimate/.
14. "Fixing the Foreign Agents Registration Act," *The Cipher Brief*, December 10, 2017, https://www.thecipherbrief.com/foreign-agents-registration-act-clearing-fog-information-war.
15. Committee to Protect Journalists, "Russia's RT Network Says It Complied with US Order to Register as Foreign Agent," November 13, 2017, https://cpj.org/2017/11/russias-rt-network-says-it-complied-with-us-order-.php.
16. Craig Timberg, Tony Romm and Elizabeth Dwoskin, "Lawmakers Agree Social Media Needs Regulation, but say Prompt Federal Action is Unlikely," *Washington Post*, April 11, 2018, https://www.washingtonpost.com/business/technology/lawmakers-agree-social-media-needs-regulation-but-say-prompt-federal-action-is-unlikely/2018/04/11/d3ce71b0-3daf-11e8-8d53-eba0ed-2371cc_story.html?utm_term=.9569cfbe7cd0.
17. Mary Clare Jalonick and Barbara Ortutay, "Zuckerberg: Regulation 'Inevitable' for Social Media Firms," Associated Press, April 12, 2018, https://www.apnews.com/04076e945181477cb9e-08a5383528b15.
18. See, for example, Bernard Goldberg, *Bias: A CBS Insider Exposes How the Media Distort the News* (Regnery, 2001).
19. See, for example, Brian Stelter, "Three Journalists Leaving CNN After Retracted Article," CNN, June 27, 2017, http://money.cnn.com/2017/06/26/media/cnn-announcement-retracted-article/index.html.
20. Sydney J. Freedberg, Jr., "Russia, China are Outmaneuvering US: Generals Recommend New Authorities, Doctrine," *Breaking Defense*, June 15, 2018, https://breakingdefense.com/2018/06/russia-china-are-outmaneuvering-us-generals-recommend-new-authorities-doctrine/?utm_campaign=Breaking%20News&utm_source=hs_email&utm_medium=email&utm_content=63810365&_hsenc=p2ANqtz-8PsIix-oKMXMCtldbM-388w6tozyZA1GfGkj9adwk2uVPmDzn6YFsw3Ftk8q_JQ-V98X-oqI9erNRElgXycjU_gpI5FxOA&_hsmi=63810365.
21. Ibid.

CONTRIBUTORS

Ilan Berman is Senior Vice President of the American Foreign Policy Council in Washington, DC. An expert on regional security in the Middle East, Central Asia, and the Russian Federation, he has consulted for both the U.S. Central Intelligence Agency and the U.S. Department of Defense, and provided assistance on foreign policy and national security issues to a range of governmental agencies and congressional offices. He is the author of four books on national security strategy and Mideast politics, and the editor of four others, including – most recently – *The Logic of Irregular War: Asymmetry and America's Adversaries* (Rowman & Littlefield, 2017).

Robert Bole is Senior Fellow for Public Diplomacy at the American Foreign Policy Council in Washington, DC. Previously, he served at the Director of Global Strategy at the Broadcasting Board of Governors (BBG), and in that capacity oversaw the formation and execution of the BBG's global growth and development strategy encompassing its television, radio, digital and mobile platforms, comprised of five separate media organizations that reached a weekly audience of 218 million in 60+ languages in over 100 markets.

David M. Denehy is the founder of The Denehy Group, a boutique international affairs consultancy. Mr. Denehy possesses over two decades of experience in international affairs, having worked in the public and private sectors in Eurasia, South Central Asia, the Middle East and North Africa. From 2013 to 2018, Mr. Denehy was the Senior Advisor on the Middle East and Libya Resident Country Director for the International Republican Institute. He has held multiple positions within the U.S. Department of State, including Senior Advisor in the Bureau of Near Eastern

Affairs, Senior Advisor and Acting Deputy Assistant Secretary in the Bureau of Democracy, Human Rights and Labor.

Dr. Aykan Erdemir is a senior fellow at the Foundation for Defense of Democracies. Between 2011 and 2015, he was a member of the Turkish Parliament, and served on the EU-Turkey Joint Parliamentary Committee, the EU Harmonization Committee, and the Ad Hoc Parliamentary Committee on the IT Sector and the Internet. Dr. Erdemir is a founding member of the International Panel of Parliamentarians for Freedom of Religion or Belief (IPPFoRB), and a recipient of the 2016 Stefanus Prize for Religious Freedom. He is co-author of the 2016 book *Antagonistic Tolerance: Competitive Sharing of Religious Sites and Spaces*, published by Routledge.

Dr. Samantha Hoffman is a Visiting Academic Fellow at the Mercator Institute for China Studies (MERICS) and a Research Consultant at the International Institute for Strategic Studies (IISS). Her research is focused on Chinese state security policy and social management. She holds a PhD in Politics and International Relations from the University of Nottingham, an MSc in Modern Chinese Studies from the University of Oxford, and BA degrees in International Affairs and East Asian Languages and Cultures from the Florida State University. The views expressed in her chapter are her own and do not reflect those of her employers.

Donald N. Jensen is a Senior Fellow at the Center for European Policy Analysis (CEPA), where he is editor of the StratCom program, and teaches in the Global Security Studies program at the Krieger School of Arts and Sciences, Johns Hopkins University. A former U.S. diplomat, he writes extensively on Russian foreign and domestic politics, especially Russia's relations with Europe. For many years, he was a senior manager at *Radio Free Europe/Radio Liberty*, where he helped that organization adapt to the challenges of the post- Cold War media environment and digital media.

Varsha Koduvayur is a senior research analyst at the Foundation for Defense of Democracies focusing on the Gulf States, where she covers internal dynamics, regional geopolitics, illicit financing, and political and economic reform trends. She was previously a researcher for the Middle East practice at the Eurasia Group, and a junior fellow at the Carnegie Endowment for International Peace.

Peter Mattis is a Research Fellow in China Studies at the Victims of Communism Memorial Foundation and a contributing editor for *War on the Rocks*. He previously worked at The Jamestown Foundation as a fellow and editor of its biweekly *China Brief*. Prior to joining Jamestown, Mr. Mattis worked as an intelligence analyst for the U.S. government and as a research associate at The National Bureau of Asian Research.

Dr. Jonathan Schanzer, a former terrorism finance analyst at the U.S. Department of the Treasury, is senior vice president for research at the Foundation for Defense of Democracies. A former research fellow at the Washington Institute for Near East Policy, Dr. Schanzer has studied Middle East history in four countries. The author of three books on the Middle East, Dr. Schanzer has testified regularly before Congress and publishes widely in the American and international media.

Merve Tahiroglu is a research analyst at the Foundation for Defense of Democracies (FDD), focusing on Turkey's foreign policy and domestic politics. Merve has published and co-authored pieces in various outlets such as *Foreign Affairs*, the *Washington Post*, the *Wall Street Journal*, *Politico*, the *Huffington Post* and *Foreign Policy*, in addition to FDD-linked publications such as The Long War Journal and Military Edge. She earned her MA in history from Georgetown University, and her BA in political science from Duke University.

Dr. Haroon K. Ullah serves as Chief Strategy Officer at the Broadcasting Board of Governors, an $800+ million global media agency. He is an award-winning author, scholar, diplomat and policy practitioner who advised three Secretaries of State, with a special focus on digital strategy, countering violent extremism and transmedia engagement. He teaches at Georgetown University. and has served as a Harvard University Belfer Fellow, a William J. Fulbright Fellow, a Harvard University Presidential Scholar, and a Woodrow Wilson Public Service Fellow. He is the author of *Digital World War: Islamists, Extremists, and the Fight for Cyber Supremacy* (Yale University Press, 2017).

Lightning Source UK Ltd.
Milton Keynes UK
UKHW020312130219
337169UK00009B/525/P

9 781538 119907